NORTH LOGAN CITY LIBRARY

I0406299

18.4
ibbo
5/6/03

Put Off
Thy Shoes

TED GIBBONS

Maasai, Inc.
Provo, Utah

NORTH LOGAN CITY LIBRARY
475 East 2500 North
North Logan, UT 84341
435-755-7169

Put Off Thy Shoes
Copyright © 2001 by Ted Gibbons
All rights reserved.

No part of this book may be used or reproduced in any manner without written permission.

Published by Maasai, Inc.
201 East Bay Blvd
Provo, Utah 84606

Front cover graphic design by Douglass Cole, Orem, Utah.
Page Layout and Design by www.SunriseBooks.com

2001 edition by Maasai, Inc.
Library of Congress Control Number: 2001099082
ISBN: 1-889025-08-9

Other Titles by Ted Gibbons

AMEN! An Interrupted Prayer
Brigham Young and the Robin Soup
Daniel Webster and the Blacksmith's Fee
Lincoln and the Lady
The Samaritan
The Talking Cat
Rending the Veil of Heaven
Misery and Joy
This Life is a Test
I Witnessed the Carthage Massacre, Audio Cassette, Video
Sealing the Testimony
The Road to Carthage
Modern Fables: Stories that Stick (with S. Michael Wilcox)

For "H" and Lola,
who showed me the way.

Table of Contents

Preface

A close friend tried to get in touch with the President of the United States a few months ago. You will not be surprised to learn that he was unsuccessful. I have no idea how many layers of bureaucracy there are between a Dallas doctor and the Oval Office, but I am certain he did not penetrate many of them. His efforts were doomed before he reached for the phone.

But God's door is always open. His line is never busy. He never has matters of such urgency that he cannot visit with us.

Directing a universe of incomprehensible size, and presiding over worlds without number, our Heavenly Father is never too busy to share a quiet, intimate, meaningful moment with his children. He has encouraged us to come *anytime*. In fact he has often directed us to call on him *all the time*. And he has promised ro respond.

> Ask, and it shall be given you; seek, and ye shall find; knock, and it shall be opened unto you... (Matthew 7:7).

This book is a manual for those who ask and seek and knock, for all those who "put off [their] shoes" and step onto the holy ground of prayer. (See Exodus 3:5.)

God Hears;
God Answers

Chapter 1

I stared into the white froth of the river as the water tumbled over the rocks and debris and raced under the bridge. Tears gathered in the corners of my eyes and slid down my face and into the torrent below. I had looked at the river, laughed, shaken my head, and my glasses were gone.

It was no more than a city creek, but heavy with spring run-off. And my glasses were in it. I stared through amblyopia and myopia into the plunging swirl, but there was nothing. After a moment, I scrambled down the bank and into the water, bending, reaching, feeling, bracing my nine-year-old body against the current. The churning of the water made it impossible to see anything. My blind groping was useless. The glasses were gone.

Finally I climbed back to the sidewalk and stood there dripping, gathering the courage to go home and tell my parents that my carelessness had once again cost them money.

Forty minutes later mother and I stood together where I had stood alone. "Did you see where they fell?" she asked.

I pointed to the spot, a white whirlpool of water, stones and sticks.

"Did you look?" she continued.

"I got into the water. That's why I'm wet, Mom. But there was no way to find them. Look at it. You can't see anything in there, and the water's going so fast they might be at the gravel pit by now." I was sobbing, surrendering to my emotions. I hated to be in trouble, and I was in trouble a lot. I hated to lose things, and I lost things all the time. Dad said I was the only kid in Logan that could clean his room in the morning and lose his bed by lunch. And I dreaded telling Dad.

Dad worked so hard to support our family. In early summer he sold garden seeds over a three-state route out of the back of a '53 Buick. In August he supervised teen-age pickers in the bean fields. The rest of the year he taught school. Our budget wasn't built to withstand my constant assaults.

"Ted..."

I looked at her again.

"Did you pray?" she asked.

I had not. I knew the words and the formalities of prayer, and I went through them regularly, but I did not expect answers. What answers were there for things like

"Heavenly Father, bless the missionaries," or "bless the poor and the sick and the needy and the afflicted," or "help me to be a good boy today." I guessed God took care of the missionaries, and watched over the unfortunate, but I never seemed to manage to be a good boy, and I never expected real answers.

"Come on, Teddy," she said. "Hold my hand. Will you ask Heavenly Father to help us?"

I took her hand as I looked at her. Her eyes were already closed, and in my heart a quiet voice whispered "She gets answers." I felt something small and warm moving in me, drying up the sadness. I bowed my head and squeezed my eyes shut.

"Heavenly Father, I lost my glasses. Daddy can't afford new ones and I need 'em to see good and do good, do better, in school. Will you please help us find them? Name of Jesus, Amen."

Mom gave me a pat on the bottom and I climbed down the bank again and waded into the water to the spot where the glasses had disappeared. I plunged in my hand and grasped a handful of sticks. After a moment's hesitation, I drew them from the water and examined them. My glasses were there, secured by the temple among twigs and rubble.

The small, warm thing in me grew then, as I stood in the water. It grew and became a shining certainty saying in me "God hears; God answers."

❧

Obstacles

Chapter 2

But when ye pray, use not vain repetitions, as the hypocrites do: for they think that they shall be heard for their much speaking (Matthew 6:7).

* * * * *

"The First Principle of the Gospel"

Joseph Smith spoke a great deal about effective prayer. On one occasion he made this observation:

> "It is the first principle of the Gospel to know for a certainty the Character of God, and to know that we may converse with him as one man converses with another..." (*Teachings of the Prophet Joseph Smith*, p.345).

That the Prophet Joseph should place on this knowledge so high a priority tells us much about the importance of our personal communication with the Father. But *knowing* is not enough. There are obstacles between knowing

and doing. Perhaps no other gospel activity is so easily mis-
managed. My prayers are not unlike my golf swing. A huge
variety of things can, and without careful attention, do go
wrong. Consider the following stories.

The first comes from Daniel V. McArthur who remembered having lunch with Joseph Smith.

When noon came we were all called to dinner at
Joseph's house. The table was loaded down with corn-
meal mush and milk, and at the bidding of Joseph we
all stepped forward to our places around the table,
standing on our feet. Joseph asked Joshua Holman, who
was one of the wood haulers, to ask a blessing upon the
food. He went at his duty with all his soul. As he had
been a Methodist exhorter before joining the Church,
he commenced to call upon the great and mighty God
who sat upon the top of a topless throne, to look down
and bless the food and asked many other blessings to
rest upon the Prophet, etc. As soon as he closed Brother
Joseph said, "Brother Joshua, don't let me ever hear you
ask another such a blessing;" and then before we took
our seats he stated his reasons for making this remark,
and showed us how inconsistent such ideas were, and
told us many things about God and who He was.
(Backman, Milton V. Jr., and Keith W. Perkins, ed.
Writings of Early Latter-day Saints and Their Contemporaries,

A *Database Collection*. Excerpts. 2nd ed., rev. and
enlarged. Provo, Utah: Religious Studies Center, 1996).

Joshua Holman found himself receiving instruction
from the Prophet because something was wrong with the
way he prayed. Clearly the obstacles to effective prayer are
not to be solved by eloquence alone.

Elder George A. Smith shared the following:

> I recollect a gentleman who came from Canada,
> and who had been a Methodist, and had always been in
> the habit of praying to a God who had no ears, and as a
> matter of course had to shout and halloo pretty loud to
> make him hear. Father Johnson asked him to pray in
> their family worship in the evening, and he got on such
> a high key, and hallooed so loud that he alarmed the
> whole village. Among others, Joseph came running out,
> saying, "What is the matter? I thought by the noise that
> the heavens and the earth were coming together," and
> said to the man, "that he ought not to give way to such
> an enthusiastic spirit, and bray so much like a jackass."
> Because Joseph said that, the poor man put back to
> Canada, and apostatized; he thought he would not pray
> to a God who did not want to be screamed at with all
> one's might (*Journal of Discourses*, Vol. II, p.214).

Again the Prophet gave instruction. The obstacles to communication with the Father through prayer are not overcome by praying loudly.

I began to experience some of these obstacles when I was a child. A lovely Sunday School teacher spoke to my class about vain repetitions. I resolved to do something about my prayers. I had a memorized sequence and memorized words. That night my dad asked me to take the lead in the family prayer. I thought for a moment of my resolve and then consciously made a change in the prayer I had offered so often. After the "Amen," I sat at the table, well-pleased with myself. An older brother, who seemed to know my prayer as well as I did, eyed me a moment and then asked, "How come you left out the part about the missionaries?"

"A Man Highly Favored"

What names come to mind when you contemplate the personalities in the scriptures and ask, "Who really knew how to pray?" Abraham? Nephi, the grandson of Helaman? Enos? Alma the younger? Joseph Smith? In any such list the name of Mahonri Moriancumer, the brother of Jared, would be prominent.

Consider the record. In Ether 1, when the languages of the earth began to be confounded, Jared came to his brother and said to him, "Cry unto the Lord, that he will not confound us that we may not understand our words" (Ether 1:34). Jared himself was a man of spiritual depth. He believed in God and knew that God answered prayers. He acknowledged the hand of God in the terrifying affairs then transpiring in the world. No doubt he prayed himself. But when he perceived a need that required the direct intervention of the Lord, he asked his brother to make the request. One is led to wonder what events had occurred in this family to create such an awareness.

Whatever the reasons, Jared knew that his brother was "a man highly favored of the Lord" (Ether 1:34), a man who got answers. The brother of Jared called upon the Lord for Jared and for the blessing he had requested, and "the Lord had compassion upon Jared; therefore he did not confound the language of Jared...and his brother" (Ether 1:35).

Jared was back shortly with another request to be channeled through his brother to the Lord. He asked his sibling to plead with the Lord again for "their friends, that [the Lord] confound not their language." The brother of Jared prayed for these friends, and "they were not confounded" (Ether 1:36-37).

The Lord had also sworn that people should be scattered all over the world (Ether 1:33). Jared, knowing this, made yet another request of his brother: "Go and inquire of the Lord whether he will drive us out of the land, and if he will drive us out of the land, cry unto him whither we shall go" (Ether 1:38).

In response to this appeal, the Lord promised to "go before [them] into a land which is choice above all the lands of the earth" (Ether 1:42).

Responding to the further supplications of Mahonri Moriancumer the Lord provided plans for the building of transoceanic barges with a ventilation system (Ether 2:16, 20). He touched the stones prepared by the brother of Jared to light the barges (Ether 3:6), and then, because of the faith of this amazing man, the brother of Jared was permitted to see the spirit body of Christ (Ether 3:13).

Saying Prayers or Praying?

In all of Holy Writ there are few if any whose petitions to the Throne of Grace were so blessed. And yet the brother of Jared did not *pray*. No form of the word "pray" can be found anywhere in the account of this man's communications with God. In fact, in the entire book of Ether, a derivative of the word "pray" appears only once, as Moroni, who abridged the book of Ether, talks about a personal experience (Ether 12:36). This is not coincidence. In his own writings, comprising 12 chapters, Moroni used some form of the word *pray* eighteen times, but he never used it in his descriptions of the brother of Jared nor in his abridgement of the Jaredite record. From that abridgement we learn that Mahonri Moriancumer *cried* to the Lord (Ether 1:35, 37, 39, etc), *called* upon the name of the Lord (Ether 2:15), *inquired* of the Lord (Ether 1:38), and received marvelous answers. But he never *prayed*.

We go through the formalities of prayer so often that there is danger of our falling into the snare of using *vain repetitions*. The Savior cautioned against this kind of praying—praying with the attitude that God will hear and answer us simply because of our "much speaking" (3 Nephi 13:7), or our much eloquence, or our much noise.

Moroni clarified the issue: "And likewise also is it counted evil unto a man, if he shall pray and not with real intent of heart; yea, and it profiteth him nothing, for God receiveth none such" (Moroni 7:9).

Perhaps in our personal and family worship we should remember the brother of Jared and consider a change in terminology. It is possible that if we change the way we talk about prayer, we can change the way we feel about it, and then the way we do it. Years ago, after a reading of the book of Ether, I tried some different words as my family knelt for family prayer. I said, "Joshua, will you say 'Good Morning' to our Father in Heaven for us?"

A moment of silence followed. Then my fourteen-year-old said, "What?"

"Will you say 'Good Morning' to our Father in Heaven for us and share with him our family's needs and thanks?" I urged.

"You mean 'say the prayer.' Right, Dad?"

"Yes, son. That's what I mean."

"Well then, why don't you say so?" he asked. He muttered something under his breath and offered our family prayer, using the phrases that have become so commonplace, so repetitive (dare I say '*vain*'?), in our family.

A Place Called Moriancumer

Perhaps even the brother of Jared started "saying prayers" (even though he called them something else), rather than "praying." Following an arduous journey through the wilderness, the Jaredites made a seashore camp in a place they called Moriancumer (Ether 2:14).

The seashore must have been a lovely respite from the trials of travel through unknown lands, transporting flocks, fowls, fish, and bees, crossing uninhabited lands, and many waters with barges they had to build themselves (Ether 2:1-3, 5-6).

The scriptures suggest that Moriancumer was a lovely place. The circumstances may have been delightful enough to cause even the brother of Jared to forget (or postpone), his quest for the most choice of all lands on earth. The record refers to mountains and trees, and there must have been fertile soil and vegetation, and an abundance of food for men and animals (Ether 6:4).

Moroni tells us in the Book of Ether of the Lord's insistence in the wilderness that this colony not stop when they found a nice place but continue their trip to the Promised Land (Ether 2:7); he then editorializes about that land. (See Ether 2:8-12.) When he returns to his narrative, he tells us that upon their arrival at the seashore, the Jaredites did the very thing they had been forbidden to do in the wilderness. They stopped (Ether 2:13).

They knew they were to go on. The fact that they spent four years in tents "upon the seashore" (Ether 2:13), indicates their awareness of a journey that must one day continue. But they made no effort to cross, or even to learn how to cross, the ocean. At the end of that time the Lord came again to the brother of Jared and talked with him for three hours. He "chastened him because he remembered not to call upon the name of the Lord" (Ether 3:14). A repentant Mahonri Moriancumer called upon the Lord then, and was told to "Go to work..." (Ether 2:15-16), and cross the ocean.

It does not seem reasonable that the brother of Jared stopped praying, although such a thing is possible. It is more likely that he stopped crying and calling. He stopped *conversing*. In the absence of great needs and problems, no necessity existed for great answers and so there were no great prayers. Life was simple. Everything was fine.

How much like that we are! We have food on the table, a roof over our heads. The doctor is a phone call away. We have money in the bank, and two cars in the garage. When the crises come, we become intense, our prayers nearly volcanic in their intensity. But in the absence of trouble, we are often satisfied with a few warm whispers. Perhaps we, like the brother of Jared, need a three-hour session with the Lord.

Joseph Smith gave a superb example of how we ought to pray. We are indebted to Daniel Tyler for this account.

At the time William Smith and others rebelled against the Prophet at Kirtland, I attended a meeting...where Joseph presided. Entering the school house a little before the meeting opened and gazing upon the man of God, I perceived sadness in his countenance and tears trickling down his cheeks. A few moments later a hymn was sung and he opened the meeting by prayer. Instead of facing the audience, however, he turned his back and bowed upon his knees, facing the wall. This, I suppose, was done to hide his sorrow and tears.

I had heard men and women pray—especially the former—from the most ignorant, both as to letters and intellect, to the most learned and eloquent. But never until then had I heard a man address his Maker as though He was present listening as a kind father would listen to the sorrows of a dutiful child. Joseph was at that time unlearned, but that prayer, which was to a considerable extent in behalf of those who accused him of having gone astray and fallen into sin, was that the Lord would forgive them and open their eyes that they might see aright. That prayer, I say, to my humble mind, partook of the learning and eloquence of heaven. There was no ostentation, no raising of the voice as by enthusiasm, but a plain conversational tone, as a man would address a present friend. It appeared to me as though, in case the veil were taken away, I could see the Lord standing facing His humblest of all servants I had ever seen. It was the crowning of all the prayers I ever heard. (In Hyrum and Helen Mae Andrus, *They Knew the Prophet*, pp.51-52).

How often do we kneel at the table or the bed and speak from habit rather than from our hearts? How often do we engage in a ritual rather than a conversation with our Father? How often do we *say our prayers* rather than converse with the Lord?

Knowing that we, like the Jaredites, are all involved in a journey to a "far better land of promise" (Alma 37:45), and that we must cross not the ocean but "an everlasting

gulf of misery which is prepared to engulf the wicked"
(Helaman 3:30), how crucial it is that we never stop com-
municating, that we never stop praying with real intent, but
that we "converse with him as one man converses with
another" as we seek the Lord's help in traveling "a strait
and narrow course..." until we can "land [our] souls, yea,
[our] immortal souls, at the right hand of God in the kingdom of heaven...to go no more out" (Helaman 3:29-30).

In the Presence of the Father

Chapter 3

Then shall ye call upon me, and ye shall go and pray
unto me, and I will hearken unto you. *And ye shall seek me,
and find me*, when ye shall search for me with all your heart
(Jeremiah 29:12-13, emphasis added).

* * * * *

Holy Ground

Jeremiah's promise that if we search diligently for the
Father we will find him is more than prophetic rhetoric.
Abraham discovered it was true!

> Now, after the Lord had withdrawn from speaking
> to me, and withdrawn his face from me, I said in my
> heart: Thy servant has sought thee earnestly; now I have
> found thee... (Abraham 2:12).

Elder Bruce R. McConkie taught

> We approach Deity in the spirit of awe, reverence, and worship. We speak in hushed and solemn tones. We listen for his answer. We are at our best in prayer. *We are in the divine presence* (Bruce R. McConkie, *Ensign*, January 1976, p.12, emphasis added).

"We are in the divine presence" when we pray. We are not sending letters or postcards. We are not leaving messages on an answering machine or flinging handfuls of beautiful words into the cosmos. We make our petitions in person, before the Throne of Grace.

Many places inspire awe and reverence. But nothing else is like this *holy ground!* We are not in the Oval Office, nor in the courts of kings, nor in the Sistine Chapel. We are in the company of the Creator. "Put off thy shoes from off thy feet," the Lord said to Moses, "for the place whereon thou standest is holy ground" (Exodus 3:5).

At the very least, as we enter the "holy ground" of prayer to the King of the Universe, we should do the same: we should pause spiritually and "take off our shoes." A private audience with God needs preparation.

> "And as surely as Christ liveth he spake these words unto our fathers, saying: Whatsoever thing ye shall ask

the Father in my name, which is good, in faith believing that ye shall receive, behold, it shall be done unto you" (Moroni 7:26).

Was there ever a promise given that embraced more joy and opportunity than this? How could we fail to prepare for such an opportunity? Some of our preparation and communication might follow this pattern:

> Now, picture him in your mind's eye. Think to whom you are speaking, control your thoughts—don't let them wander, address him as your Father and your friend. Now tell him things you really feel to tell him— not trite phrases that have little meaning, but have a sincere, heartfelt conversation with him. Confide in him, ask him for forgiveness, plead with him, enjoy him, thank him, express your love to him, (Elder H. Burke Peterson, *Conference Report*, Oct 1973, p.13).

"The Spirit of Awe"

What if this note came to you by special courier? "You are requested to meet with the President of the Church at the time and place of your choosing. The full resources of the Church are available, and you have permission to ask for anything."

How much time would you spend in laying the ground-work for such a meeting? What kind of thoughts would go into your requests? What would your attitude be?

Can you imagine yawning or dozing off in such a meeting? Would you race through the formalities and then leave so that you could get on to *more important* matters?

We have just such an request from the God of the universe. The brother of Jared demonstrated how we ought to regard an invitation to meet with the our Heavenly Father.

> O Lord, thou hast said that we must be encompassed about by the floods. Now behold, O Lord, and do not be angry with thy servant because of his weakness before thee; for we know that thou art holy and dwellest in the heavens, and that we are unworthy before thee; because of the fall our natures have become evil continually; nevertheless, O Lord, thou hast given us a commandment that we must call upon thee, that from thee we may receive according to our desires (Ether 3:2).

Is our own entrance into the Father's presence typified by this same demeanor? Do we rejoice at the privilege he has granted us to counsel with him? I have teenagers who love me very much, but who believe the major purpose of my existence is to meet their needs. "Hey, Dad!" they say as they run into the room, "Can I borrow five bucks?" or "Do you need the car tonight?" I love them but their approach is wrong.

Yet many of us approach our Heavenly Father in the same way. We fall to our knees between the nightly news and bed, pour out a sufficient collection of thoughts to justify the effort, and go to sleep.

I was in the hall of the Mission Home of the Brazilian Mission as a young missionary. Someone told me that Elder Spencer W. Kimball was in the President's office interviewing missionaries. He had no schedule. Anyone in the hall was likely to get a turn. I sat down and waited by the door. I was filled with anticipation. I was about to have a personal meeting with an apostle of the Lord.

Imagine yourself in the hallway outside the office of God, waiting for the door to open, waiting for your turn to meet with him. That is the feeling we should bring to prayer. Calling upon God *always* demands preparation.

"The Sacred Language"

Part of the process of entreating the Father in a proper manner is addressing him in what Elder L. Tom Perry called "the sacred language of prayer" (*Conference Report*, October 1983, p.14).

When we go to worship in a temple or a church, we put aside our working clothes and dress ourselves in something better. This change of clothing is a mark of respect. Similarly, when we address our Heavenly Father, we should put aside our working words and clothe our prayers in special language of reverence and respect. In offering prayers in the English language members of our Church do not address our Heavenly Father with the same words we use in speaking to a fellow worker, to an employee or employer, or to a merchant in the marketplace. We use special words that have been sanctified by use in inspired communications, words that have been recommended to us and modeled for us by those we sustain as prophets and inspired teachers (Elder Dallin H. Oaks, *Conference Report*, April 1993, p.17).

"But this is unfamiliar and difficult," some might say. Elder Oaks continues:

Why should we have to use words that have not been in common use in the English language for hundreds of years? If we require a special language of prayer in English, we will discourage the saying of prayers by little children, by new members, and by others who are just learning to pray.

Brothers and sisters, the special language of prayer is much more than an artifact of the translation of the scriptures into English. Its use serves an important, current purpose. We know this because of modern revelations and because of the teachings and examples of modern prophets. The way we pray is important (Elder Dallin H. Oaks, *Conference Report*, April 1993, p.17-18).

In the Name of Jesus Christ

Chapter 4

I cried unto him continually, for he had said unto me: Whatsoever thing ye shall ask in faith, believing that ye shall receive in the name of Christ, ye shall receive it (Enos 1:15).

* * * * *

"A Family Name"

The name of Christ is a family name, and it is appropriate that those who have taken upon them this name refer to each other by family titles. We greet each other as "Brother" and "Sister" so routinely that the profound meaning of our salutations escapes us. But King Benjamin made it clear when he said,

> And now, because of the covenant which ye have made ye shall be called the children of Christ, his sons and his daughters; for behold, this day he hath

spiritually begotten you; for ye say that your hearts are changed through faith on his name; therefore, ye are born of him and have become his sons and his daughters...I would that ye should take upon you the name of Christ, all you that have entered into the covenant with God that ye should be obedient unto the end of your lives (Mosiah 5:7-8).

In the Lord's instructions for the School of the Prophets, he directed that members should greet each other with these words:

Art thou a brother or brethren? I salute you in the name of the Lord Jesus Christ, in token or remembrance of the everlasting covenant, in which covenant I receive you to fellowship.... (D&C 88:133).

As sons and daughters of the Savior, spiritually begotten of him, we who have made the covenants receive a family name and refer to each other as "Brother" and "Sister" in the family of Jesus Christ. As family members we are empowered to pray in his name—the family name— when we petition the Father.

"Use My Name"

Many years ago I joined two of my older brothers, both of them doctors, for a sealing in the Mesa, Arizona Temple. The oldest brother had adopted an infant and had waited the required amount of time. The child was now to be sealed to him and his wife. I was there with another brother to witness the ceremony.

We spoke in the dressing room. The middle brother was within weeks of leaving the Army, where he had served out a commitment he had incurred for financial assistance received during his medical training. We both wondered what his plans would be after his discharge.

"I wanted to go to work in a clinic in Dallas, Texas," Larry said, and he named the clinic. "But I called and the secretary refused to put me through to the director. What a shame. It would have been a great place to practice."

The older brother looked delighted and responded, "Larry, I know the man who runs that clinic. He and I are friends. Write to him. Use my name. Ask for an interview. I'll call him and tell him of our relationship."

Larry did write, using the name of his older brother, and did get an interview and did get the position he wanted. The Savior has invited us to use his name in the same way. This is a wonderful blessing to us, for a unique relationship exists between the Father and the Son. Notice the language of the Father when he speaks of Jehovah:

At the time of the baptism of Jesus, the Father said, "This is my beloved Son in whom I am well pleased" (Matthew 3:17).

On the Mount of Transfiguration the Father said, "This is my beloved Son in whom I am well pleased; hear ye him" (Matthew 17:5).

In the Sacred Grove the Father said, "This is My Beloved Son. Hear Him!" (Joseph Smith–History 1:17).

In the land Bountiful in 34 AD the Father said, "Behold my Beloved Son, in whom I am well pleased, in whom I have glorified my name–hear ye him" (3 Nephi 11:7).

Isaiah gave us more of the Father's words about his Son: "Behold my servant, whom I uphold; mine elect, in whom my soul delighteth" (Isaiah 42:1).

Jehovah has been perfect in obedience and submission, "the will of the Son being swallowed up in the will of the Father" (Mosiah 15:7). He is a "beloved" son, in whom the Father is "well pleased," in whom the Father's soul "delighteth;" a son to whom was given "from God the Father honor and glory" (2 Peter 1:17). The use of this name in our prayers matters, and we are invited, even commanded, to petition the Father in the name of this divine being who is our elder brother.

Behold, I say unto you that whoso believeth in
Christ, doubting nothing, whatsoever he shall ask the
Father in the name of Christ it shall be granted him;
and this promise is unto all, even unto the ends of the
earth (Mormon 9:21).

The Savior has in effect said to us, "When you petition
the Father for the blessings you need, for help with the trials you face, for revelation and inspiration and comfort, use
my name. You have my permission. Use my name."

"Let All Mem Beware"

A word of caution is necessary about this matter. In
D&C 63:61-63 the Lord warns, "Wherefore, let all men
beware how they take my name in their lips. For behold,
verily I say, that many there be who are under this con-
demnation, who use the name of the Lord, and use it in
vain, having not authority. Wherefore, let the church
repent of their sins, and I, the Lord, will own them...."

The actual language of the ten commandments does
not refer to swearing, that is, profanity, but to this very
principle: "Thou shalt not take the name of the Lord thy
God in vain" (Ex. 20:7).

We must speak Christ's name in our prayers with reverence and gratitude. With what other perspective could
we possibly approach God the Father and appeal to him in

the name of his Only Begotten Son, in whom he is well pleased?

Real Intent

Chapter 5

And likewise also is it counted evil unto a man, if he shall pray and not with real intent of heart; yea, and it profiteth him nothing, for God receiveth none such (Moroni 7:9).

* * * * *

"Prayers and Works"

Enos teaches an interesting lesson about prayer with the words he uses to describe his own supplications. The key words and phrases are in italics:

"I will tell you of the *wrestle* which I had before God" (1:1)

"I *cried* unto him in *mighty prayer* and supplication" (1:4)

"I did *pour out my whole soul* unto God" (1:9)

"While I was thus *struggling in the spirit*" (1:10)

"I prayed unto him with *many long strugglings*" (1:11)

"After I had prayed and labored with all diligence" (1:12)

"I cried unto him *continually*," (1:15)

Patricia T. Holland observed:

> We are [adults] now, not children, and we are
> expected to pray with maturity. The words most often
> used to describe urgent, prayerful labor are wrestle,
> plead, cry, and hunger. In some sense, prayer may be the
> hardest work we ever will engage in, and perhaps it
> should be (*Ensign*, Oct. 1987, p.31).

It was family reunion time and we were heading for
Utah from a small community in northeastern Arizona. As
we passed through Flagstaff, we stopped at a department
store to purchase some supplies. Acting on what I considered a whim, I decided to buy a pocket knife. I had never
carried one, and had no need to do so then, but the incli-
nation was there, and I made the purchase.

Many miles later on the reservation, and some distance
from Cameron, the car began to shudder madly. We
stopped at once and I opened the hood. I am not a
mechanical wizard. When I have car trouble, I look for an
on-off switch in the *off* position. If I cannot find one, I call
for a professional. In fact, I carry no tools in my car because
I would not know what to do with them.

It was a sweltering day, the temperature near one hundred degrees. The car held the family: my wife and me and

six kids. I did not know what to do. I tried to drive the car again. It was useless.

I explained the problem to the family. Debbie, eight, was the first to suggest prayer. We all bowed our heads. No one remembers the words, nor any particular feeling during the prayer. But when it was over, I walked once again to the front of the car and surveyed the engine compartment. An impression came. "Cut that belt." And I knew which one!

I looked at the belt for a long time. It connected two pulleys fastened to pieces of equipment whose purpose I could not understand. But the impression persisted. I leaned through the open window of the car and told my wife what I was feeling. She shared my concerns. There was simply no way to know in advance the consequences of the act. The car was already nearly undrivable, but I had no desire to make things worse.

However, because of the knife, I had the courage to proceed. Without it, such an impression would have been meaningless. I reflected a moment on the *coincidence* of purchasing the knife and my present impression to use it. I opened a blade and cut the belt. When I started the engine; the shaking ceased.

We stopped in Cameron thirty-five minutes later and talked to a mechanic. The belt had something to do with the air conditioner. By cutting it, I had disconnected a worn out bearing, nothing more. We drove on to Utah, sweating and rejoicing.

One part of receiving answers is expecting answers. Another part is being committed to the direction answers will take us. We must be willing, in the words of Enos, to "pray *and* labor." We must be willing to use the knife and cut the belt.

In the scriptures, Moroni calls such an attitude "real intent." Praying without it, he says, is evil (Moroni 7:9); but when real intent is combined with a sincere heart and faith in Christ, answers come through the Holy Ghost (Moroni 10:4).

For those who pray in such a way, the event is neither a ritual nor a vain repetition. This kind of prayer is an honest expression of the feelings of the heart, coupled with a determination to get answers *and* to apply them. Praying with real intent is always accompanied by action. We seek the Lord having done all that we can do, or we leave his presence committed to do all that we can do. Elder Bruce R. McConkie wrote that "Prayer and works go together. If and when we have done all we can, then in consultation with the Lord, through mighty and effectual prayer, we have power to come up with the right conclusions" (*Ensign* January 1976, p.12).

A friend taught me this lesson. We met while we were in the Army in North Carolina and my wife and I invited my friend and his wife into our home to be taught the Gospel. They accepted our invitation.

By the end of the first discussion, the wife was converted. The Spirit had borne witness to her and she was ready to be baptized. But her husband, John, could get no such confirmation. He continued to attend the discussions; he prayed and we prayed with him and for him. We fasted in his behalf and implored the Lord to touch his heart. He liked the Church and was impressed with its organization and leadership, but he could not get an answer to his prayers. His wife made the decision to postpone her baptism until her husband was ready to join her. And so the weeks passed, a continuing cycle of apparently unanswered prayers.

Then one Sunday following sacrament meeting John announced that his prayers had been answered. He asked to be baptized.

"What happened?" we inquired, and he told us. He had been praying constantly about the Church and Joseph Smith and the Book of Mormon, but always with this feeling: "Once I know if it is all true, *then* I will decide whether or not to repent and accept baptism." But the knowledge never came. Then, during sacrament meeting that day one of the speakers delivered a message that answered some questions about the Church that John had discussed with his wife the night before. His heart was touched. His spirit responded.

During the closing prayer of the meeting he said his own prayer: "Lord, if thou wantest me to be baptized, tell me and I'll get up and go do it now." He reported to us that before he could say "Amen," he received his answer. Finally, he had prayed with real intent. He was not just saying, "I really want to know." He was saying, "I will go and do."

"With A Sincere Heart"

Moroni's injunction that we pray about the Book of Mormon with real intent is his warning to us that no witness will come unless we are determined, *in advance*, to obey the teachings of the book if it is true. This is an important principle in all of our communication with God. Unless we are resolved to obey, we may seek answers in vain.

Without this willingness to do whatever is necessary, we will never pray with much success. With the resolution to work, we will find our communication with God infused with great power. It is because of this intrinsic bond between works and prayers that Amulek concluded his message on prayer by saying:

And now behold, my beloved brethren, I say unto you, do not suppose that this is all; for after ye have done all these things, if ye turn away the needy, and the naked, and visit not the sick and the afflicted, and impart of your substance, if ye have, to those who stand in need—I say unto you, if ye do not any of these things, behold your prayer is vain, and availeth you nothing, and ye are as hypocrites who do deny the faith" (Alma 34:28).

Prayers and Potatoes

On November 30, 1856 this principle came to life for some church members in Utah. The day was Sunday and the Salt Lake saints were assembled that morning in the Tabernacle. Brigham Young had just been informed that members of the overdue handcart companies who had suffered so much in the snows of Wyoming were about to arrive. He said,

The afternoon meeting will be omitted, for I wish the sisters to go home and prepare to give those who have just arrived a mouthful of something to eat, and to wash them and nurse them up. You know that I would give more for a dish of pudding and milk, or a baked potato and salt, were I in the position of those persons who have just come in, than I would for all your prayers, though you were to stay here all the afternoon and pray.

Prayer is good, but when baked potatoes and pudding and milk are needed, prayer will not supply their place... (Reported in the Salt Lake *Deseret News*, December 10, 1856, p.320).

Friends watched the same kind of thing happen in the small town of Taylor, Arizona. The community was threatened with flooding. The rains had continued for days, the river was rising, and homes and property were in jeopardy. By Sunday they knew the water was coming. They did not meet in sacrament meeting to pray for relief and protection. The ox was already in the pit (Luke 14:5). They prayed. They prayed a lot. But they also dressed in their work clothes and filled sandbags.

Inherent in the process of praying with real intent is the willingness to work. We must be willing to do whatever is required to receive the answer we seek, and whatever is necessary to comply with it.

"What Will Ye That I Should Do"

In response to divine direction, the brother of Jared had supervised the construction of eight barges in which his colony would cross the ocean to America. But there were three problems with these ships: there was no way to steer them; because they were airtight, those who journeyed in them would not be able to breathe; and since there was no light within, they would not be able to see.

Mahonri took these problems and "cried unto the Lord."

With regard to the first problem, the Lord promised to do the steering:

> For behold, ye shall be as a whale in the midst of the sea; for the mountain waves shall dash upon you. Nevertheless, I will bring you up again out of the depths of the sea; for the winds have gone forth out of my mouth, and also the rains and the floods have I sent forth. And behold, I prepare you against these things; for ye cannot cross this great deep save I prepare you against the waves of the sea, and the winds which have gone forth, and the floods which shall come (Ether 2:24-25).

Christ solved the problem of lack of air by giving Jared's brother the design for a ventilation system. He told his servant to knock a hole in the top and the bottom of each boat and to put a cork in each hole. "When you need air, take out the cork. If water comes in, close it quick." (See Ether 2:18-20.)

This mighty man went to work and ventilated the boats according to the instructions he had received. Then he cried to the Lord again about the darkness within the vessels.

The Lord's response was unexpected: it is as though he said, *What do you want me to do?* "What will ye that I should prepare for you that ye may have light?" (Ether 2:23).

There is a logical answer to this question: "I want you to solve the light problem like you solved the other problems." But for the brother of Jared, who had prayed with *real intent,* the Lord's question was a call to work. This time the work preceded the answer he wanted. And he worked with what seems to be perfect confidence in the answer he expected to receive. This account is a stirring witness of the faith for which this man is renowned.

How much thought and effort must have gone into his plan! Shining stones must have seemed an excellent solution to the Jaredite prophet. That God who is the light of the sun, the moon, and the stars could certainly be a source of light for a few small stones. The brother of Jared did not do the easiest thing, however. He did not scurry around on the seashore looking for sixteen rocks, and then ask the Lord to touch them. He must have known that the power of God would be sufficient to light any rock. But he was not interested in asking God to touch just any rock.

He seems to have known what he was looking for. He went to Mount Shelem, so called because of its exceeding height (Ether 3:1), and found a rock of special composition. How much effort was required to get to the mountain? How high did he climb and how long did he look to find the rock he needed? When he found it, "he did molten...sixteen small stones," white, clear, and transparent like glass (Ether 3:1). How much toil was there in this work? But with the stones prepared, he still was not finished, for "he did carry them in his hands upon the top of the mount." (The exceedingly high mountain!) Then, and only then, having done all that he could possibly do and having done it with as much care and skill as he could, he "cried again unto the Lord..." (Ether 3:1), and told the Lord what he wanted him to do.

The answer to that prayer is one of the most moving answers to prayer ever given in the history of this world.

We must, if we desire to converse with the Father, make a similar effort. We must fortify our prayers with works and thereby demonstrate our faith in God's ability and willingness to answer. When we know what we want God to do, we must proceed with great faith as we prepare for him to do it.

Lost Keys

A Seminary teacher shared this experience. He awoke at 4:15 a.m. one morning with a project to complete in the classroom before his first class. As he walked past his dresser on the way to the shower, he discovered that his keys were not there. He searched in the logical places, and then in the less likely ones, but without success. There would be no point in going to the building at 5:00 if he could not get in, and he felt that it was too early to awaken another teacher to borrow keys.

He knew of only one thing to do. He knelt and explained his need to his Father in Heaven. A question came into his mind: "How can I let the Lord know that I believe he will help me find my keys?"

The brother of Jared showed his confidence in the Lord by preparing in advance for the answer he hoped to receive. But how could this teacher show the Lord that he believed he could get divine help in finding the keys? He showered, shaved, dressed in his suit, and filled his brief-case, ready to go to work, and knelt again. He had prepared himself in every way for the answer he anticipated. "Father," he began, and a memory came. He saw himself the night before, running across the back yard in the dark-ness. He had stepped in a hole and fallen to the ground. "Thanks, Father," he said. He went to the back yard, picked up the keys from where they had slipped from his pocket, and went to work.

Fourteen Dollars

My wife and I shared a similar experience. We were married while we were in college. We had agreed during our courtship that we would not postpone having children. I had a full-time, night-shift job. We would work hard, save where possible, and trust the Lord that we could make it financially.

We talked often about how narrow a margin we would have for the unexpected. "Sweetheart, what will we do if the time comes when we simply do not have enough to get by?" I asked one Sunday as we sat in the swings of an elementary school. The wedding was only a few weeks away.

"We'll trust the Lord," she said.

"How?" I wanted to know. "How will we demonstrate that kind of trust?"

"What does your mother do when she is in financial difficulty?" she asked me. "Does she pay less tithing?"

"No," I answered. "She pays more."

"We can do something like that," she continued. "If the time ever comes when can't meet our needs, we will take whatever we have, donate it to the Lord, tell him our needs, and trust him."

Two years went by. We had a baby and another one was coming. Medical bills and car repairs had left us with fourteen dollars in the bank. We needed fifty. The next paycheck was a week and a half away.

We talked at the kitchen table one Saturday afternoon. "Do you remember what we decided?" my bride asked me.

I remembered. But that was talk. We were down to our last fourteen dollars with no prospect for more for at least ten days.

"Sweetheart," my wife said, "we made a covenant. The Lord has never let us down. He won't now."

We wrote a check for fourteen dollars the next morning, made out to the ward building fund, and then told the Lord that we needed fifty dollar and that we trusted him.

Even so, I spent my time in Sunday School and Priesthood meeting trying to decide how to get by without any money for a week and a half.

As we entered our apartment after church, the phone was ringing. It was my mother. We visited for a moment, and then she asked,

"Son, do you remember in elementary school when you used to take a quarter or two each week and buy stamps to fill up U.S.Savings Bonds?" she asked.

I had a vague recollection. It had been a long time.

"I was in the basement this morning," she continued, "and I opened an old box. I saw an envelope in the top of it. In the envelope were the two bonds you bought in 1954 and 1955. Let's see. That would be second and third grade."

"What denomination are they?" I asked, and I felt that small, warm thing moving in me.

"They are 25-dollar bonds," she said. "They are past maturity, of course, and must be worth a little more than fifty dollars."

Jesus said, "For your Father knoweth what things ye have need of, before ye ask him" (Matthew 6:8). Did he know when I was in the second grade that one day my wife and I would need fifty dollars and pray for it with real intent? Of course he did. The Lord made this promise: "And it shall come to pass, that before they call, I will answer..." (Isaiah 65:24).

Moroni, when he spoke of real intent, also enjoined "a sincere heart" and "faith in Christ" (Moroni 10:4). We must have sincerity and faith as we pray. It seems improbable that the fifty dollars would have been found in that box if my wife and I had held on to the fourteen dollars until my mother called. The keys would probably have remained in the yard for some time if the teacher had prayed in his pajamas, thinking, "If I don't find those keys, I'll go back to bed and sleep a couple of hours." Likewise, if the brother of Jared had prayed and said, "Lord, what about shining stones? Would that work? If I went and found some pretty rocks, couldst thou touch them and cause them to shine for lights in the boats?" As a result of that kind of attitude, the trip across the ocean might well have been conducted in darkness.

How Much Time?

How long does it take to pray with real intent? Those who approach the Lord with sincerity and real needs are not bound by constraints of time. They pray until they have accomplished the purposes of their prayers. Praying with real intent takes as long as it takes.

There is no value in multiplying words without meaning of course. President Joseph F. Smith taught

> I say to my brethren...do not go beyond what is wise and prudent in fasting and prayer. The Lord can hear a simple prayer, offered in faith, in half a dozen words, and he will recognize fasting that may not continue more than twenty-four hours, just as readily and as effectually as He will answer a prayer of a thousand words and fasting for a month (*Conference Report*, October 1912, p.134).

During the early days of Church history, Heber C. Kimball sought lodging and food from a widowed member of the Church. She offered what she could: a meal and a room. When he went off to bed, an idea came to her, and she thought, "Here's my opportunity...I would like to find out what an apostle says when he prays to the Lord." She made her way quietly to his room and put her ear next to the closed door. She listened as Brother Kimball sat down on the bed. She heard the thump as each of his shoes hit the floor. The springs creaked as he leaned back on the bed. Then he spoke these words: "Oh Lord, bless Heber; he is so tired." (See "Are General Authorities Human?" *The New Era*, January 1973, p.33.)

To be evaluated, this prayer must be seen in context as the expression of a man who has centered his whole day in service, obedience, and (no doubt), prayer. There is no shame in being so exhausted with honest toil that a lengthy prayer is impossible, particularly if a person recognizes prayer as a blessing rather than a duty.

On occasion I have prayed in this way: "Heavenly Father, I love thee. I am so tired tonight. Please watch over me and my family as we sleep. I will visit with thee in the morning." Such a prayer seems to be a better choice than trying to communicate with my brain so fogged with weariness that sleep or wandering thoughts are almost a certainty.

Such a prayer is not an excuse for not praying, but a commitment to meaningful prayer. However, it is the exception, and not the rule. Great prayers, or prayers that get great answers, are often driven by longings so deep that minutes and hours are meaningless.

Enos wrote, "The words which I had often heard my father speak concerning eternal life, and the joy of the saints, sunk deep into my heart, *and my soul hungered....*"

Impelled by that hunger, Enos knelt and cried unto his Maker. "All the day long did I cry unto him; yea, and when the night came I did still raise my voice high that it reached the heavens" (Enos 1:3-4).

Speaking of these verses, Elder Harold B. Lee said,

> I once read that scripture to a woman who laughed and said, "Imagine anybody praying all night and all day." I replied, "My dear sister, I hope you never have to come to a time where you have a problem so great that you have to so humble yourself. I have; I have prayed all day and all night and all day the next day and all night the next night, not always on my knees but praying constantly for a blessing that I needed most (*The Improvement Era*, October 1966, p.898).

What could anyone say during all of that time? Enos describes his prayers as "a wrestle," and as "many long strugglings" (Enos 1:2, 11). Much of this wrestling, this struggling, must have been wordless—an effort to reach not up to God but into himself. He was not trying to get God ready to answer, but to get himself ready to receive an answer. Paul wrote, "...But the Spirit itself maketh intercession for us with groanings which cannot be uttered" (Romans 8:26), or as Joseph Smith restated this phrase: "with strugglings which cannot be expressed"

(*Teachings of the Prophet Joseph Smith*, p.278). These silent thrusts of longing may become the most powerful prayers of all.

Nephi, the grandson of Helaman, went before the Lord to plead for "those who were about to be destroyed because of their faith" in Christ (3 Nephi 1:11). This was no cool, bargaining exposition but a mighty cry for the protection of the righteous. And there was no question of giving up when the answer did not come at once. 3 Nephi 1:7-8 tells us, "And it came to pass that he cried mightily unto the Lord all that day...."

Even the Savior with his superlative powers of spirituality felt the need of continuing communication with the God of us all. When the time came for him to choose the Twelve who would share his mortal ministry, "he went out into a mountain to pray, and continued all night in prayer to God" (Luke 6:12).

"More Earnestly"

After his resurrection, as a glorified and perfected being, Christ still prayed to the Father. The Book of Mormon recounts an unforgettable experience when the surviving descendants of Lehi heard the Savior pray unto the Father for them:

The eye hath never seen, neither hath the ear heard, before, so great and marvelous things as we saw and heard Jesus speak unto the Father;

And no tongue can speak, neither can there be written by any man, neither can the hearts of men conceive so great and marvelous things as we both saw and heard Jesus speak (3 Nephi 17:16-17).

However, it was in the Garden of Gethsemane, as he anticipated the agony of the atonement and the unspeakable burden of the sins of all men, that the Savior set a magnificent example for all those who suffer and struggle and weep. "My soul," the Savior said, "is exceeding sorrowful, even unto death" (Matthew 26:38).

He asked the disciples to watch and wait, and then went several yards away and prayed. Three times he bowed before his father under the weight of an increasing anguish. "And being in an agony, *he prayed more earnestly*" (Luke 22:44, emphasis added). This perfect being, who partook finally of the fulness of his Father (D&C 93:12-13), prayed, in his hour of greatest trial, "more earnestly."

"*What Could Be Wrong?*"

Sometimes responses come after many prayers rather than after one extended prayer. This experience is also a function of praying with real intent, but it can be discouraging unless we recognize the Lord's right to answer in the way and at the time that will be of most benefit to us, and unless we acknowledge his right to say "No."

Boyd K. Packer said,

> Sometimes you may struggle with a problem and not get an answer. What could be wrong?
>
> It may be that you are not doing anything wrong. It may be that you have not done the right things long enough. Remember, you cannot force spiritual things.
>
> Sometimes we are confused simply because we won't take no for an answer (*Ensign*, November 1979, p.21).

In General Conference of 1944. Joseph F. Merrill of the Council of the Twelve shared a personal experience with prayer.

> When I was about ten years of age, I began to pray for a special blessing. But I did not get an answer...no answer came...and so I continued to pray, feeling that when I could make myself worthy of an answer, I would get it.... In the latter part of August, 1887, in my nineteenth year, *after I had been praying nightly for nine long years with all the earnestness of my soul for this special blessing,* I was alone in the bedroom, and I said, half aloud,

"O Father, wilt thou not hear me?" I was beginning to get discouraged.

Then...something happened. The most glorious experience that I have received, came. In answer to my question I heard as distinctly as anything I ever heard in my life the short, simple word, "Yes."

Simultaneously my whole being, from the crown of my head to the soles of my feet, was filled with the most joyous feeling of elation, of peace and certainty that I could imagine a human being could experience. I sprang from my knees, and jumped as high as I could, and shouted, "O Father, I thank thee." At last an answer had come. I knew it (*The Improvement Era*, May 1944, pp.281-282, emphasis added).

Prayers that get answers must be offered with real intent. We must pray about real needs and real problems, not ignoring the matters of general and continuing concern, but never limiting our prayers to them. We must be willing to invest the time required for us to accomplish his purposes. We must expect answers, and we must be willing to go in whatever direction the answers take us. Sometimes we must proceed on the basis of faith, as if we had received the answer already.

A desire to be led by the Lord is a strength, but it needs to be accompanied by an understanding that our

Heavenly Father leaves many decisions for our personal choices. Personal decision-making is one of the sources of the growth we are meant to experience in mortality. Persons who try to shift all decision making to the Lord and plead for revelation in every choice will soon find circumstances where they pray for guidance and don't receive it. For example, this is likely to occur in those numerous circumstances where the choices are trivial or where either choice is acceptable. We should study things out in our mind, using the reasoning powers our creator has placed within us. Then we should pray for guidance and act upon it if we receive it, and upon our best judgment if we do not. Persons who persist in seeking revelatory guidance on subjects on which the Lord has not chosen to direct us may concoct an answer out of their own fantasy or bias, or they may even receive an answer through the medium of false revelation (Elder Dallin H. Oaks, "Our Strengths Can Become Our Weaknesses," BYU Fireside, June 7, 1992).

Giving Thanks

Chapter 6

But ye are commanded in all things to ask of God, who giveth liberally; and that which the Spirit testifies unto you even so I would that ye should do in all holiness of heart, walking uprightly before me, considering the end of your salvation, doing all things with prayer and thanksgiving... (D&C 46:7).

* * * * *

"He Did Sing Praises"

The brother of Jared, rejoicing in his experiences with Christ (Ether 3-5), had a sense of gratitude. As he and the Jaredites journeyed across the ocean, sometimes above the water and sometimes below (Ether 6:6-8), this inspired leader and his people did not simply plead for survival; they spent their time in thankful prayer.

And they did sing praises unto the Lord; yea, the brother of Jared did sing praises unto the Lord, and he did thank and praise the Lord all the day long, and when the night came, they did not cease to praise the Lord (Ether 6:9).

Our prayers almost always include gratitude, but often these expressions are memorized sentiments that originate in the mind rather than in the heart. We do not often "sing praises" to the Lord out of a fullness of joy and gratitude. We do not often seek an audience with our Father in Heaven just to say "Thanks."

Spiritual self-esteem begins with the realization that each new morning is a gift from God. Even the air we breathe is a loving loan from him. He preserves us from day to day and supports us from one moment to another. (See Mosiah 2:21.)

Therefore, our first noble deed of the morning should be a humble prayer of gratitude. Scripture so counsels: "Pray unto God, and he will be favourable unto [you]: and [you] shall see his face with joy" (Job 33:26; see also Alma 34:21; 37:37).

I did not fully appreciate the significance of prayerful greetings until I became a father myself. I am so grateful that our children never gave their mother or dad the silent treatment. Now I sense how our Heavenly Father may appreciate our prayers, morning and night. But I can imagine the pangs of his sorrow because of silence from any of his children. To me, such ingratitude seems comparable to sullen goldfish oblivious to kind providers who sprinkle food in their bowl. Indeed, those who pray can "worship God with exceedingly great joy" (Alma 45:1; Elder Russell M. Nelson, *Ensign,* Nov. 1986, pp.68-69).

This message from Elder Nelson about gratitude is not unlike one shared by Elder A. Theodore Tuttle:

We had spent nearly four years in South America and returned just in time for our eldest son to enter Brigham Young University. Several months after school had begun we received a call—I think it was a collect call—and the conversation proceeded something like this:

"Hello, Dad?"

"Yes."

"This is David."

"Yes, what do you want now?"

"Oh, nothing."

"Nothing! Well, why did you call then?"

"Oh, I just wanted to tell you about school. I love it. It's great. I am glad to be here. I like the place where I live. I like my roommate. I like the professors and I like the spirit here."

And I said, "Yes, but what do you need?"

"I don't need anything."

"Well, why did you call?"

"I just called to say 'Thank you.' I am grateful for your helping me to be here."

Well, there was considerable silence on our end of the line and we muttered something about, "We're glad you're happy." Later that night as his mother and I prayed, we thanked the Lord for a thankful son. The lesson of course came clear to me. I appreciate a son who says, 'Thank you' for things that parents have done, as all parents do. But I am a son also. I have a Father in heaven, who, like me, appreciates a son or a daughter who frequently says, "Thank you" (*The New Era*, June 1972, p.11).

"Ten Men That Were Lepers"

This is the lesson of the story of the ten lepers in Luke 17.

> And as he entered into a certain village, there met him ten men that were lepers, which stood afar off....

They were at the entrance to the village rather than within. Their disease prevented them from close society with any but their own kind. Thus, when they spoke to the Savior, they "stood afar off."

And they lifted up their voices and said, Jesus, Master, have mercy on us.

And when he saw them, he said unto them, Go shew yourselves unto the priests.

Leviticus 14 gives the laws for the cleansed leper, and the primary requirement was a visit to the priest. Going now became an act of faith, for they were directed to go toward the house of the priest as if they were already healed, trusting the power of the Savior to heal them at a distance. They went.

And it came to pass, that, as they went, they were cleansed.

Visualize this experience. These men who had lived with the reality of their uncleanness found themselves in an instant whole and new. It was as though a terminal cancer had not simply gone into remission but had disappeared in an explosion of ecstasy. Their joy must have transcended expression. Thinking only of a return to their families and loved ones, they sped to the house of the priest.

Except one.

And one of them, when he saw that he was healed, turned back, and with a loud voice glorified God, and fell down on his face at his feet, *giving him thanks...*

And Jesus answering said, were there not ten cleansed? but where are the nine?

There are not found that returned to give glory to God, save this stranger (Luke 17:12-18, emphasis added).

We can understand the emotion driving the nine ex-lepers homeward because most of us would have been with them. But this "stranger" teaches an important lesson. As we enjoy the rewards of God's goodness, we ought to fall at his feet and give him thanks. The Lord said, "And he who receiveth all things with thankfulness shall be made glorious" (D&C 78:19). Not just happy; not just healed. Glorious.

An old legend tells the story of two angels who were sent from the presence of God. Each was given a basket. One was instructed to gather requests and the other to gather thanksgivings. The angel who collected requests came back with a basket stuffed and overflowing. The angel of thanksgivings came back with a basket nearly empty. If these two angels were to listen to you and divide your prayers between them, which of them would fill his basket first?

"I Began A Fast"

My Mother spent much of my childhood on her knees. She was not giving thanks, she was praying for strength. I was trouble with a capital "T." Dad always said I was the rock-throwingest kid in the history of America, and there were broken windows and cracked windshields enough to prove it. When I discovered that Mom liked flowers, I picked three hundred tulips from the neighbor's yard and delivered them to her. I shut down a construction company one weekend when I discovered that the workers left the keys with the equipment and added them to my key collection.

Still, I loved the Church and looked forward to my mission. After several months in the field, I wrote home to tell Mom that I had been called to a leadership position. I thought she would be proud. She began her response like this: "When I got your last letter, I began a fast...."

A fast? "Why a fast?" I thought. I wrote home once to tell my mother that I was going to have a routine physical examination. She put my name on the temple prayer roll. Now she had received a letter containing what she should have considered good news, and she fasted! Her letter continued: "...because I wanted to get as close as I could to my Father in Heaven, so that I could tell him how grateful I am for what he has done for you in your life." She fell on her face at his feet, giving him thanks.

"In Every Thing Give Thanks"

When Ammon saw the Spirit being poured out upon the hitherto ferocious and iniquitous Lamanites, according to his prayers, "He fell upon his knees, and began to pour out his soul in prayer and thanksgiving to God..." (Alma 19:14).

President Joseph Fielding Smith taught:

> In our prayers we should pour out our souls in thanksgiving for life and being, for the redeeming sacrifice of the Son of God, for the gospel of salvation, for Joseph Smith and the mighty work of restoration brought to pass through him. We should acknowledge the hand of the Lord in all things and thank him for all things both temporal and spiritual (*The New Era*, September 1971, p.40).

King Benjamin, in responding to the love and gratitude of his people, said, "If I...do merit any thanks from you, O how you ought to thank your heavenly king" (Mosiah 2:19).

In our dispensation the Lord has instructed, "Thou shalt thank the Lord thy God in all things" (D&C 57:7).

This verse adds an interesting dimension to gratitude. We must do more than give thanks for the good things, the warm and pleasant blessings, the merciful generosity of God. We must give thanks for everything. Even fleas.

Corrie and Bessie Ten Boom were prisoners in the Ravensbruck Concentration Camp in Nazi Germany. They had a Bible, and in their daily study they read the words of Paul: "In every thing give thanks: for this is the will of God in Christ Jesus concerning you" (1 Thessalonians 5:18). On the day that they read that passage, they had been assigned to a new barracks. It was incredibly crowded, impossibly filthy, and it was swarming with fleas. These sisters determined to deal with their despair by thanking God for every possible thing about their new location. Corrie, at Bessie's urging, took the lead. She thanked the Lord for their being assigned together, for the Bible they had, and for the crowding in the barracks so that Christ's story could be shared with more people. Then Bessie told her sister to thank God for the fleas.

It seemed absurd, perhaps insane,and probably sacrilegious, but the scripture said "every thing," and so Corrie stood there in that filthy place and thanked God for fleas.

They soon learned that their barracks offered unusual freedoms to them, more than they had ever known in any other camp or building. They were able to read and teach the Bible to many of those who were with them. Guards and supervisors refused to enter the building. Several days passed before they discovered the reason: the fleas. (*The Hiding Place*, by Corrie Ten Boom, pp 198-209.) "And in nothing doth man offend God, or against none is his wrath kindled, *save those who confess not his hand in all things*, and obey not his commandments" (D&C 59:21, emphasis added). We must confess his hand, we must acknowledge his goodness. We must continually give thanks.

We must remember in our relationship with our Father that "It is a good thing to give thanks to the Lord, and to sing praises unto [his] name, O Most High: To shew forth [his] lovingkindness in the morning, and [his] faithfulness every night" (Psalm 92:1-2).

D&C 133 speaks of the time of the Second Coming, a time when "the presence of the Lord shall be as a melting fire...when the mountains will flow down...and...the sun shall hide its face and the moon shall withhold its light...the stars shall be hurled from their places...for this was the day of vengeance..." (D&C 133:41, 44, 49, 51).

But in the midst of this cataclysmic destruction we are told what will be *mentioned* by the faithful.

> And they shall mention the loving kindness of their
> Lord and all that he has bestowed upon them according
> to his goodness, and according to his loving kindness,
> forever and ever (D&C 133:52).

We probably ought not to wait for his arrival to mention these things, however. We ought to communicate our thankfulness now in our prayers of gratitude.

◈

Praying Vocally

Chapter 7

I kneeled down before my Maker, and I cried unto him in mighty prayer and supplication for mine own soul; and all the day long did I cry unto him; yea, and when the night came I did still raise my voice high that it reached the heavens (Enos 1:4).

* * * * *

"I Will Lift Up My Voice"

Joseph Smith described the religious controversy in his region as a "war of words and tumult of opinions" (Joseph Smith–History 1:10). He wanted desperately to know the truth, but he did not know how to find it. When it was evident that there was no other place to go, he made the decision to follow the counsel of James and ask God which of all the churches was true. It is meaningful to note that when Joseph offered this heartfelt plea for light and direction, for the first time in his life he prayed out loud.

It was on the morning of a beautiful, clear day, early in the spring of eighteen hundred and twenty. It was the first time in my life that I had made such an attempt, for amidst all my anxieties I had never as yet made the attempt to *pray vocally* (Joseph Smith–History 1:14, emphasis added).

Praying vocally should be an important part of our association with our Father in Heaven. Most personal prayers, at least among those with whom I am acquainted, are secret, silent prayers. There are advantages to praying in this way. No one is disturbed. Sensitive concerns can be communicated. Such prayers can be offered at any time and in any place.

Obviously, secret prayer is necessary in many cases where it is awkward or infeasible to pray vocally. So, if we are in a social or a business setting and need comfort or direction, a resort to secret prayer is often our only alternative (Francis M. Gibbons, "The Dual Aspects of Prayer," *Ensign*, Nov. 1991, p.78).

In this same sermon, Elder Gibbons suggests another reason for silent prayer:

But a more significant reason for praying secretly is found in the D&C, section 6, where it is written, "Yea,

I tell thee, that thou mayest know that there is none else save God that knowest thy thoughts and the intents of thy heart" (D&C 6:16).

...God has provided a channel of communication between him and his children on earth that Satan, our common enemy, cannot invade. This is the channel of secret prayer. The significance of this to the Latter-day Saint is profound, for by this means we are able to communicate with our Heavenly Father in secrecy, confident that the adversary cannot intrude (Francis M. Gibbons, "The Dual Aspects of Prayer," *Ensign*, Nov. 1991, p.78).

Nevertheless, a careful reading of the Book of Mormon makes a strong case for vocal prayers. Without question, most of the prayers of the Book in Mormon are vocal. Consider these scriptures:

And by day have I waxed bold in mighty prayer before him; yea, my voice have I sent up on high (2 Nephi 4:24).

I will lift up my voice unto thee; yea, I will cry unto thee, My God... (2 Nephi 4:35).

He cried mightily, saying... (Alma 22:17).

And he lifted up his voice to heaven, and cried...
(Alma 31:26).

Nearly one hundred times in the Book of Mormon
some form of the verb "to cry" is used to denote prayer. A
"cry" is usually vocal. Amulek indicates this in his stirring
sermon on prayer when he counsels: "And when you do
not *cry unto the Lord*, let your hearts be full, drawn out in
prayer unto him continually" (Alma 34:27), emphasis
added). In other words, when we do not or cannot pray
vocally, then we should pray in our hearts.

Prayer is such a privilege—to speak to our Father in
Heaven. It was a prayer, a very special prayer, which
opened this dispensation! It began with a young man's
first vocal prayer. *I hope that not too many of our prayers are
silent,* even though when we cannot pray vocally, it is
good to offer a silent prayer in our hearts and in our
minds (President Spencer W. Kimball, *Conference Report,*
October 1979, p.4, emphasis added).

President Spencer W. Kimball also said:

We recall the many times the Lord instructs us to
pray vocally. "And again, I command thee that thou
shalt pray vocally as well as in thy heart; yea, before the
world as well as in secret, in public as well as in private"

(D&C 19:28). So central is this to our prayers and personal religious life that the Lord instructed the priesthood brethren to "visit the house of each member, exhorting them to pray vocally and in secret and attend to all family duties (*Ensign*, October 1981, p.2).

Helam

From the experience of the people of Alma at Helam comes this episode. The Nephites who had been baptized at the Waters of Mormon and who had settled at Helam were placed in bondage by the Lamanites. (See Mosiah 18, 23, 24.) Amulon, Alma's former colleague and present enemy, was made king over the people of Alma, and he made their lives miserable. He "exercised authority over them, and put tasks upon them, and put taskmasters over them" (Mosiah 24:9).

> And it came to pass that so great were their afflictions that they began to cry mightily to God.
>
> And Amulon commanded them that they should stop their cries; and he put guards over them to watch them, that whosoever should be found calling upon God should be put to death (Mosiah 24:10-11).

In the bitterness of his apostasy, Amulon installed the death penalty for vocal prayer. Therefore:

Alma and his people did not raise their voices to the Lord their God, but did pour out their hearts to him; and he did know the thoughts of their hearts (Mosiah 24:25).

Since they could not pray aloud, they prayed in their hearts. The Lord responded,

Lift up your heads and be of good comfort...I will deliver [you] out of bondage. And I will ease the burdens which are put upon your shoulders (Mosiah 24:13-14).

Haun's Mill

An account of a similar incident comes from the massacre at Haun's Mill in 1838. Nineteen men and boys were killed in the attack on a small Mormon settlement by a mob of Missouri settlers. Fifteen others were wounded. The mob, before leaving, "pillaged the village and robbed the dead of their boots, clothing, and valuables." When they left the mill "they dragged with them horses, wagons, cows, and property of nearly every description belonging to the settlement" (*Joseph Smith and the Restoration*, Ivan J. Barrett, 1968, p.330).

A few days following the attack, some of the mob returned. According to members of this group of rabble, they "lived fat, too," feasting on the remaining cattle and hogs that should have sustained the surviving widows and orphans, as well as the wounded (*Joseph Smith and the Restoration*, Ivan J. Barrett, 1968, p.330).

Like the people of Alma, these unfortunate victims found their only solace in prayer, and the widows vented their feelings in heartfelt appeals to their Heavenly Father (*Assorted Gems of Priceless Value*, N.B. Lundwall, p.97). And, like Amulon, two thousand years earlier, the mobbers responded with death threats.

One of the mob delivered the warning, "The captain [Captain Comstock] says if you women don't stop your damn praying, he will send down a posse and kill every damn one of you!" Prayers and cries were hushed as women, fearful for their lives, spoke to their Creator in the silence of their hearts.

But for at least one, this terrified silence was a shame and humiliation. Amanda Smith longed to hear her own voice raised in prayer. One morning, as the day began, she slipped into a nearby cornfield, crawled into a shock of corn, and raised her "voice high that it reached the heavens" (Enos 1:4).

As she left her sanctuary a voice spoke to her, repeating the following words from the hymn "How Firm a Foundation":

That soul who on Jesus hath leaned for repose,
I cannot, I will not desert to its foes;
That soul, though all hell shall endeavor to shake,
I'll never, no never, no never forsake!

From that moment on, she was at peace (*Assorted Gems of Priceless Value*, N.B. Lundwall, p.97).

Pray out loud as often as possible. The vocalization of prayers helps focus thoughts, and keeps the mind from wandering. Finding a place where prayers can be offered aloud will enable a person to avoid the distractions of places where people might interrupt. And as we hear our words with our ears, our faith that God will hear us with his ears will be increased.

The 77th Psalm says, "I cried unto God with my voice, even unto God with my voice; and he gave ear unto me" (Psalm 77:1).

❧

The Song of the Heart

Chapter 8

Sing praises to God, sing praises: Sing praises unto our King, sing praises (Psalm 47:6).

* * * *

"Sing Redeeming Love"

The Lord invited Emma Smith to "make a selection of sacred hymns" for use in the Church.

For my soul delighteth in the song of the heart; yea, the song of the righteous is a prayer unto me, and it shall be answered with a blessing upon their heads (D&C 25:11- 12).

The significance of music in heaven is a matter for reflection. The truth, as expressed in the verse above, is that when we sing sacred hymns from our heart, we pray. Please note that the revelation makes no mention of musical talent or of the *song of the vocal cords*. Any sacred thoughts that come from our hearts accompanied by worthy music ascend to heaven as prayers.

Alma referred to this kind of music in his sermon to the people of Zarahemla. He encouraged them to remember those who were in captivity in the Land of Nephi and who were rescued from sin and bondage by the goodness of God. "They were loosed, and their souls did expand, and *they did sing redeeming love*. And I say unto you that they are saved" (Alma 5:9, emphasis added). The Anti-Nephi Lehies were also "brought to sing redeeming love" (Alma 26:13).

It must be this longing to "sing redeeming love" that turns a song into a prayer. The scriptures are filled with examples. When Christ came among "an innumerable company of the spirits of the just" in the Spirit World to deliver them from the bands of death (D&C 138:12), "they sang praises to his holy name" (D&C 138:24). When Christ was about to depart from the room of the Last Supper to go the Garden of Gethsemene, he and his disciples sang a hymn. (See Matthew 26:30.) Isaiah instructed us to sing when we are resurrected. "Awake and sing, ye that dwell in dust...the earth shall cast out the dead" (Isaiah 26:19).

> And the graves of the saints shall be opened; and
> they shall come forth and stand on the right hand of the
> Lamb, when he shall stand upon Mount Zion, and

upon the holy city, the New Jerusalem; and they shall sing the song of the Lamb, day and night forever and ever (D&C 133:56).

Israel sang after they had crossed the Red Sea. "I will sing unto the Lord, for he hath triumphed gloriously..." (Exodus 15:1). The D&C gives the words of a song to be sung, a new song, when the time comes that "all shall know me, who remain, even from the least unto the greatest..." (D&C 84:98; the words of the song are in verses 99-102).

Making Sounds; Making Music

At least forty-six times the scriptures speak of singing praises to the Savior and other members of the Godhead.

And he hath brought to pass the redemption of the world, whereby he that is found guiltless before him at the judgment day hath it given unto him to dwell in the presence of God in his kingdom, to sing ceaseless praises with the choirs above, unto the Father, and unto the Son, and unto the Holy Ghost, which are one God, in a state of happiness which hath no end (Mormon 7:7).

We must not miss opportunities to sing redeeming love—to sing praises—because of *how* we sing. The quality that matters in music is *why* we sing.

I sang with the Utah State University Institute Choir at a session of General Conference many years ago. I had what I thought was the misfortune to be seated next to a young man who sang every note off-key and every note as loudly as he could! I am sorry to confess that I was offended. Even with my limited musical ability I recognized that I was making a much more useful contribution to the spirit of our music than he was. I have since learned that I had the matter exactly backwards.

Alexander Schreiner, one of the great Tabernacle organists, recalled a story about someone who asked a music director how he could stand to hear Brother Stanton bellow off-key at Church gatherings. The wise old leader replied:

> Brother Stanton is one of our most devout wor-shippers, and when he bellows he is a supreme musi-cian.... Don't pay too much attention to the sounds he makes. If you do, you may miss the music (*Music and the Gospel*, p.16; cited in the *Ensign*, March 2000, p.19).

I was so worried about the sounds I was hearing that I missed the music I was hearing. I am certain that our

Father never pays too much attention to the *sounds* we make. If we are devout in our worship, God does not hear the missed notes or care about the dissonance. He hears the prayers.

> When we listen to this choir...we listen to music, and music is truth. Good music is gracious praise of God. It is delightsome to the ear, and it is one of our most acceptable methods of worshipping God. And those who sing...should sing with the spirit and with the understanding. They should not sing merely because it is a profession, or because they have a good voice; but they should sing also because they have the spirit of it and can enter into the spirit of prayer and praise to God who gave them their sweet voices (Joseph F. Smith, *Conference Report*, Oct. 1899, p.69).

The Old Testament contains a splendid story about an extraordinary use of music. When Jehosaphat was king in Jerusalem, an alliance of armies from Moab, Ammon, and Mount Seir came to battle against Judah. The king proclaimed a fast among his people, for he knew that his people had "no might against this great company..." (2 Chronicles 20:12).

The Lord by revelation promised them protection. "Be not afraid nor dismayed by reason of this great multitude," he encouraged. "Ye shall not need to fight in this battle: set yourselves, stand ye still..." (2 Chronicles 20:15, 17).

The next morning they arose and went to meet the invading forces, armed with *music!*

> And when he had consulted with the people, he appointed singers unto the LORD, and that should praise the beauty of holiness, as they went out before the army, and to say, Praise the LORD; for his mercy endureth for ever.
>
> And when they began to sing and to praise, the LORD set ambushments against the children of Ammon, Moab, and mount Seir, which were come against Judah; and they were smitten (2 Chronicles 20:21-22).

Heavenly Music

The scriptures make it clear that there is singing in heaven. Both Lehi and Alma saw multitudes of angels "in the attitude of singing and praising their God" (I Nephi 1:8; Alma 36:22). Instrumental music must be a part of this, even in celestial regions. It also seems clear that in mortality instrumental music played from the heart to praise and proclaim redemption becomes a prayer.

Melvin DeWitt, a wonderful man and a fine musician shared a missionary experience in a stake conference which I attended.

Elder Henry D. Moyle of the Quorum of the Twelve had heard Elder DeWitt play his violin in a missionary meeting. He invited Elder DeWitt to tour the mission with him and his wife and play the violin.

> He explained that his wife was too timid to speak, but loved to participate by contributing musically in the conference, and accompanying me on the violin would make it appropriate for her.

Elder DeWitt was pleased to accept that assignment. During a testimony meeting with the missionaries of the St. Louis District in the basement of a government building, Elder DeWitt had just decided to stand and express his feelings when Elder Moyle stood and said to him, "Elder DeWitt, will you please bear your testimony on the violin?" Elder DeWitt wrote,

> This startled me and I wondered at first what he meant. Then the thought came clear to me–Yes, this is what you actually do when you play from your heart...While I was puzzling in my mind what to play (alone without accompaniment–for there was no piano

there), Brother Moyle suggested that I play "Oh, My Father." He said he would like to hold the hymn book for me to play from.... The Holy Ghost came to me and filled my whole being with the most heavenly influence. I began to play and I never heard such sounds come from my violin. Tears of joy began to roll down my cheeks. I also saw tears running off Brother Moyle's cheeks. There came to my awareness that a heavenly orchestra was accompanying me, so wonderful and completely beyond anything musical you would ever hear on this mortal earth....

[Then] Brother Moyle began to speak and bore witness that we were entertained by heavenly beings... (by Elder Melvin K. DeWitt; personal correspondence to the author).

Elder Jeffrey R. Holland told of an inactive man who was reclaimed by an experience in the shed behind his house. In terror he had fled there, although he did not know the source of his fear. For the first time in half a century, he fell to his knees and prayed: "O Lord, save me from whatever it is that terrifies me so."

Quaking, trembling, perspiring on his knees in this shed out behind his home, he continued his prayer. He said, "I was lisping like a child the only prayers I knew, when there came into my heart the words of a song that

I had not heard nor sung for that half century. I think I did not ever know the words, and I surely do not know them now. But I heard them with symphonic accompaniment and angelic choirs. I heard them, music and word, in that shed behind my home in the middle of that night.

The hymn was "We Thank Thee, O God, for a Prophet."

The man said,

I heard the angels sing. I've never missed a church meeting since that day. I've never smoked a cigarette, and I've tried to do everything I should have done for all those years. But I want you to know that I did not then, and probably do not now know, the words to the hymn that I heard sung that night in a shed behind my home with celestial symphony and an angelic choir (From a speech by Jeffrey Holland, "Remembered and Nourished by the Good Word of God," given at the Marriott Center, BYU, Sept. 26, 1976).

Praying in Unison

Music allows us to pray together, as do our congregational and family prayers.

I will now ask this congregation, how many of you thought of mentally repeating my prayer as the words came to your ears? Did you realize that the order of prayer required you to mentally follow the words of the person who was praying? With us every one should mentally repeat the same words and ask for the same things as does the one who leads vocally, and let all say, amen. There are times and places when all should vocally repeat the words spoken, but in our prayer meetings and in our family circles let every heart be united with the one who takes the lead by being mouth before the Lord, and let every person mentally repeat the prayers, and all unite in whatever is asked for, and the Lord will not withhold, but will give to such persons the things which they ask for and rightly need (Brigham Young, *Journal of Discourses*, Vol III, p.53).

"Answered With A Blessing"

The First Presidency, in the introduction to our hymn book, said this:

Brothers and Sisters, let us use the hymns to invite the Spirit of the Lord into our congregations, our homes, and our personal lives. Let us memorize and ponder them, recite and sing them, and partake of their spiritual nourishment. Know that the song of the righteous is a prayer unto our Father in Heaven, "and will be answered with a blessing upon [your] heads" (*Hymns of the Church of Jesus Christ of Latter-day Saints*, 1985, p.x).

Listening

Chapter 9

Behold, I stand at the door, and knock: if any man hear my voice, and open the door, I will come in to him, and will sup with him, and he with me (Revelation 3:20).

* * * * *

A Telephone Prayer

Midnight was a distant memory when I awoke. My knees felt as if they had been used for anvils. As I slowly straightened my legs and climbed into bed, I was filled with remorse. I had gone to sleep while I was praying, and it was not the first time. The demands of family, work, and school, together with a chaotic schedule, had caused me to try and pray when I was so exhausted that my mind refused to focus. Even when I did not sleep, I was as likely to think of Statistics 501 or mopping the floor at Sears as I was of my Heavenly Father. The lines of my communication were frayed. It might only be a matter of time till they failed altogether. My last thought as I drifted off to sleep was that I needed to do something and that I had better do it at once.

The next evening I picked up the Book of Mormon. With a pen in hand and a notepad close by, I made my way through the book and wrote out, longhand, every passage that had anything to say about prayer. I had expected a project of a week, but this effort required more than a month.

It was an astonishing adventure. I found more information about prayer than I had ever imagined was in the Book of Mormon, and more insights than I could have hoped for. The material was complex, but also cohesive. The patterns and purposes of prayer were unfolded in clarity, with enough examples to provide me with a new motivation to communicate productively with my Father.

When I finished my search, I organized many of the scriptures I had transcribed into a logical sequence, with transitions, and then, as opportunities came, shared what I had learned.

Years passed. A mission field dream was realized when I was hired to teach in the Seminary program. One day, in a conference with my supervisor, I mentioned my experience with prayer and the Book of Mormon and shared some of the things I had learned. He seemed interested and asked me if I would make my presentation to all of the teachers in the area at our next inservice meeting. I was happy to accept that assignment.

As I wrestled to find a format for teaching my peers, my thoughts centered on the problems that hinder effective prayer. I remembered the nights I had gone to sleep on my knees near my bed. I remembered the countless times I had prayed, and then, without listening for an answer, climbed at once into bed and gone to sleep. I recognized that in the absence of impending disaster there was a redundancy in my prayers. They were almost always filled with the same daily cliches and standard phrases.

I began asking myself some questions: What if a close friend spoke to me only once or twice a day but never gave me an opportunity to respond? What if he always said about the same things? "The trouble with many of our prayers," said President Hinckley, "is that we give them as if we were picking up the telephone and ordering gro-ceries—we place our order and hang up" (*Standing For Something*, p.116). And then an idea came.

Our Church Education System district was situated in an area with small seminaries located in a number of cites. Before the day of my presentation, I wrote a one-sided tele-phone call patterned after the prayers we so often offer. It went like this:

Hello, _____. This is Ted.

I just wanted to thank you for your help and friendship this year. As you know, I've been in charge of inservice training, and your support has meant a lot to me and made my job easier. Thanks, too, for your great example and the wonderful job you do with the young people.

By the way, our supplies for the coming year have just arrived, and we didn't get everything we need. I'd like to ask you to help us make up some shortages. We need a couple of dozen binders, a bunch of bookmarks, colored pencils, and all the scripture chase cards you can spare. Oh, and we also need Bibles. Please bring this stuff to the meeting tonight if you can.

I'll see you. Goodbye.

My intent was to call some of the teachers, read my script to them, and hang up. I would then have them share their feelings about my phone call during my instruction about prayer. I felt it was a brilliant strategy, which would assist me in teaching a powerful lesson regarding the feelings of our Heavenly Father about our "all-talk, no-listen" prayers.

On the morning of the day I was to make my presentation, while the teachers were at their respective seminaries, I went to my office and made long-distance calls to four of them.

As each teacher answered, I said, "Hello," and called him by name. I then proceeded to read the text I had written. After reciting the "thank you" section and the "needs list," I said "Goodbye" and hung up. The calls went as I had expected. Since I did not allow those I called to utter a single word except "Hello," there was little chance of a surprise. But I got one.

I had only been out of the office a minute when one of the teachers in my building called me to the phone. I was wanted by one of the men to whom I had just spoken.

I walked back to the office, picked up the phone, and said, "Hello." I proceeded to read my text once more, word for word. When I had finished, I said "Goodbye" and hung up again.

This time the phone rang before I got to the door. I answered it. "Hello?"

"Ted! What in the..."

I could tell he was upset, but I had an experiment to conduct, so I began reading the lines of my *telephone prayer* again.

I don't insist on perfection in any man. I know myself too well. Moreover, I had spent time in the Army and I had heard my share of colorful language. The words did not stop me, even though he spoke them with a fluency that gave indication of ranching or military service. Nor I did have any actual fear that his fury and frustration might lead to cardiac arrest. But he was so upset at me and at my refusal to communicate with him that I finally stopped *talking* and started *conversing.* When he was calm enough, I told him what I was doing and asked him to record his feelings so he could share them with the rest of the faculty.

I hung up the phone and sat at my desk pondering the intensity of his response. It must be a terrible disappointment to our Eternal Father when he stands at the door and knocks, and we will not hear his voice.

My message that evening went very well. The printed outline of my study of prayer in the Book of Mormon was well received. The description of my little simulation was humorous. Anticipation preceding the explanations by the teachers of their feelings about my phone calls was intense. As I listened to those four, I felt I was a part of a superb teaching moment. I was certain that I had taught a beneficial lesson about our Father in Heaven and about the necessity of listening.

But one of those four teachers taught an even better lesson: a lesson about God's love, and about his willingness to answer prayers. Following the meeting, he led me to the parking lot and opened the trunk of his car. It was full of binders and bookmarks and scriptures and scripture cards—all the things I had asked for.

"Ever So Quietly"

Once we have mastered the attitude that allows us to pray with real intent, we must discipline ourselves to listen. President Kimball said,

> But is prayer only a one-way communication? No! One of the reasons "prayer is the soul's sincere desire" (*Hymns*, no. 220), is because prayer is such a privilege—not only to speak to our Father in Heaven, but also to receive love and inspiration from him. At the end of our prayers, we need to do some intense listening—even for several minutes. We have prayed for counsel and help. Now we must "be still, and know that [he is] God" (Psalms 46:10; *Ensign*, October 1981, p.5).

Receiving answers will usually require more than simply listening, however. We live in a culture of confusion, a society where the loudest voice usually gets the most attention. But answers from the Father are not generally strident. Boyd K. Packer taught that

> "Some answers will come from reading the scriptures, some from hearing speakers. And, occasionally, when it is important, some will come by very direct and powerful inspiration. The promptings will be clear and unmistakable" (*Ensign*, November 1979, p.21).

What a thrill it would be to feel the earth tremble beneath our feet as God spoke to us in all the majesty of his infinite power in response to our petitions. But expecting such manifestations may make us deaf to the quiet knock at the door. President Spencer W. Kimball gave us this warning:

> The burning bushes, the smoking mountains.... the Cumorahs, and the Kirtlands were realities; but they were the exceptions. The great volume of revelation came to Moses and to Joseph and comes to today's prophet in the less spectacular way—that of deep impressions, without spectacle or glamour or dramatic events.
>
> Always expecting the spectacular, many will miss entirely the constant flow of revealed communication (*Conference Report*, Munich Germany Area Conference 1973, p.77).

Elder Eyring said of that quiet voice of inspiration: "Now, I testify it is a small voice. It whispers, not shouts. And so you must be very quiet inside" (*Conference Report*, April 1991, p.87).

In fact, recognizing and understanding the sweet, quiet voice of the Spirit is a skill that must be learned. Elder Packer said,

"It is difficult to separate from the confusion of life that quiet voice of inspiration. Unless you attune yourself, you will miss it. Answers to prayers come in a quiet way.... If you really try, you can learn to respond to that voice." *Ensign*, November 1979, pp.19-20).

The Sound of A Baritone

Learning to hear that voice takes practice. Near the end of my sixth grade year, the district music instructor came to our school room. He hung a chart on the wall showing all the instruments of the band and talked to us about joining his junior high band the following fall.

When the class left for recess, I went to speak to him. "I think I'd like to be in the band," I said.

"That's great!" He seemed excited. "What instrument do you play?"

I was embarrassed to tell him that I did not play any instrument and that I never had, but he did not seem to mind. "What would you like to play?"

I surveyed the chart. I wanted to make a lot of noise without working too hard. I finally pointed to a brass instrument that reminded me of a anemic tuba. "What's that?"

"That's a baritone," he responded. "It is about this big," and he held his hands three feet apart. "The band always needs good baritone players. And you wouldn't have to purchase an instrument. The district owns a few of them."

I had some concerns. "I'm not very musical," I told him, "and besides, I don't think I've even seen or heard a baritone. I don't have any idea what one sounds like."

"Not a problem," he insisted. "Everyone in the seventh grade band will be a beginner. You will learn quickly enough. And if you're really anxious to improve your skills, you can attend the section practice sessions with the advanced band."

I did. I played the baritone through three years of junior high and two years of high school. I practiced with the baritone section on a weekly basis during most of those years. Then, in my senior year, because of changing interests, I elected not to take band. In the intervening years, I have picked up and played a baritone one time.

But an amazing thing happened to me in those years when I focused time each day on what a baritone is supposed to sound like. Even now, whenever I hear a band, whether live or recorded, whether loud or soft, regardless of what other instruments are performing, if the baritones are playing I can *always* hear them. My ear has become attuned.

Elder Packer spoke of the need to expand our ability to hear the still, small voice. He talked of listening to the same whisper of inspiration both as a boy and as an apostle.

He said, "The signal is much clearer now" (*Ensign*, November 1979, p.21).

So it can be with us. Through continuing association, through careful attention, through practice and through righteous living, we can learn to hear more clearly the quiet inspiration that will come in answer to our prayers.

Two other factors influence our success in hearing and understanding answers to our prayers. They are the conditions relating to *where we pray* and *when we pray.*

Where To Pray

Prayers can be offered anywhere. Alma's sermon to the poor Zoramites makes this clear. (See Alma 33:3-11.) Many heartfelt prayers have been offered in unusual circumstances, sometimes in that instant before tragedy strikes. But in most cases, we have a measure of control over the selection of the place we choose to pray. The Savior said,

But thou, when thou prayest, enter into thy closet, and when thou hast shut thy door, pray to thy Father which is in secret, and thy Father which seeth in secret shall reward thee openly" (Matthew 6:6).

Amulek spoke of prayers over our stewardships, and for our families, and for our protection, and then said, "But this is not all; ye must pour out your souls in your closets, and in your secret places, and in your wilderness" (Alma 34:26).

When Joseph Smith offered the prayer that changed the course of human history, he "retired to the woods [his own "secret place"] to make the attempt...to the place where [he] had previously designed to go," a sacred place where he could be alone (Joseph Smith—History 1:14-15).

What purpose was served by the walk to the Sacred Grove? Why ought we to offer prayers in our closets, our secret places, our wilderness? Joseph went to be alone. A large family in a small cabin would not offer many undisturbed moments for thoughtful prayer. My own experience (and I suspect the experience of many people), is that the interruptions of television and telephone and family make interludes of quiet time a precious commodity. Sometimes we can enhance the power of our prayers by finding places to pray that are free from the noises of the world. Elder L. Tom Perry found a place in his home that meets this requirement.

> The home we have just purchased since moving west has one unique feature. The small study provided has an adjoining large closet about one-fourth the size of the entire study. We thought when we were considering the purchase of the home that this closet was an error in design. Since occupying the home, it has become one of

my favorite places. Here is where I can shut myself off from the world and communicate with my Father in heaven. "But thou, when thou prayest, enter into thy closet, and when thou hast shut thy door, pray to thy Father which is in secret; and thy Father which seeth in secret shall reward thee openly" (Matthew 6:6; *Conference Report*, April 1973, p.16).

President Kimball indicated that we ought to locate a place to which we can go and pray vocally, as Joseph Smith did. He said,

"I have long been impressed about the need for privacy in our personal prayers.... We, too [like Joseph Smith], ought to find, where possible, a room, a corner, a closet, a place where we can 'retire' to 'pray vocally' in secret" (*Ensign*, October 1981, p.4).

When To Pray

We must also consider *when* we pray. It is possible that a prayer offered in the moments before sleep by the side of the bed presents some challenges to communication. After a hard day's labor wrestling children or professional problems, the proximity of the bed may be a narcotic. Moving to another room—the living room if the house is quiet, the

NORTH LOGAN CITY LIBRARY
475 East 2500 North
North Logan, UT 84341
435-755-7169

back yard, the study, even the bathroom—may enhance the quality of our prayers.

The importance of when and where we pray was taught to me many years ago by an Institute teacher. I was dating the girl who is now my wife, and I was in love. I had no question about my feelings. But the prospect of eternity was sobering. I needed to know the Lord's will before I entered a commitment destined to last millions of years. I prayed constantly for divine verification of my feelings, and there were days when I was certain. But there were other days, dark days, when I wrestled with doubt. So I visited my Institute teacher.

"What you need, Ted," he counseled, "is to get an answer you can rely on, an answer that comes while you are under the influence of the Holy Spirit. Once you have that direction, you do not need to worry about how you feel when you are faced with finals and research papers and the concerns of your education and demands of your work, when the cares of the world intrude upon the affairs of your heart."

He advised me to go to the temple. "Go early," he counseled, "and go when you have nothing else to do for the evening. Attend a session, get yourself in tune with the Spirit, and then stay in the temple, pondering and praying, until you have your answer. When that answer comes, build your life around it."

I cleared my calendar for an evening and attended an early-afternoon session. When I left the building late that night, I was at peace. The unmistakable impression of the Spirit was this: "If you are willing, if you are worthy, your relationship with this daughter can be an eternal one." Days still came when there were doubts, but they did not paralyze me. I had prayed **where** I could feel the Spirit and be free from interruptions, and I had prayed **when** there was nothing to pull me away from my purpose.

Answers

Chapter 10

Ask, and it shall be given unto you; seek, and ye shall find; knock, and it shall be opened unto you. For every one that asketh, receiveth; and he that seeketh, findeth; and to him that knocketh, it shall be opened (3 Nephi 14:7-8).

* * * * *

"Seek, And Ye Shall Find"

Have you noticed that there is no uncertainty in the way the Lord speaks to us about answers to our prayers? Clearly conditions exist which affect our productivity in praying, but when the Lord speaks of giving answers, he never leaves us in doubt about what he will do. Not a single verse on prayer with which I am acquainted contains conditional language. The Lord has never said, "Ask and *maybe* you will receive. Seek and ye *might* find. Knock and *perhaps* I will open unto you."

The verb of divine choice with regard to answers to our prayers seems to be *shall,* and we ought to remember it.

God Answers Every Prayer

If we are willing to acknowledge that "No" is an answer, then we must acknowledge that the Lord answers every prayer, and that he answers either in the way we want, or in a better way, "for every one that asketh receiveth" (Matthew 7:8). The form of the answer is determined by God's desire to bring to pass our immortality and eternal life (Moses 1:39), and not alone by our desires. And regardless of his response, we must be assured that he will listen and give us the answer that is best for us. He may not always give us what we want, but he will always give us what we need. The presence of God is like a "sea of glass and fire where all things...are manifest past, present, and future, and are continually before the Lord" (D&C 130:7). It is on the basis of that all-knowing perspective that God listens and answers. It must be interesting for him to evaluate our requests, based on the perspective we gain by standing on anthills while he views us from the heights of the mountains.

There seem to be at least three answers that our Father can give.

1. Yes. It will be good for you. You have asked in the name of my Son. You have asked with real intent.

2. No. It's not good for you. It will not bless you. I want you to grow.

3. Wait. Not yet. You aren't ready.

To these possible answers might be added a fourth:

4. It does not matter. Decide for yourself and I will support you in your decision.

When we pray for something we want, we seek answer number one. When the other responses come, unless we are submissive and certain of God's love, and unless we have confidence in God's perspective, we may have feelings of betrayal or unworthiness.

It is so hard when sincere prayer about something we desire very much is not answered the way we want. It is especially difficult when the Lord answers "No" to that which is worthy and would give us great joy and happiness. Whether it be overcoming illness or loneliness, recovery of a wayward child, coping with a handicap, or seeking continuing life for a dear one who is slipping away, it seems so reasonable and so consistent with our happiness to have a favorable answer. It is hard to understand why our exercise of deep and sincere faith from an obedient life does not bring the desired result (Elder Richard G. Scott, *Ensign*, Nov. 1995, p.16).

I remember a time when I had such feelings.

My father died when I was seventeen and my mother lived for nineteen years as a widow. Then she remarried. She and her new husband lived in Logan, Utah, a couple of hours away from my home in Orem. A few years after her second marriage, her new husband passed away. She had by that time become almost completely blind, but she was fiercely independent and refused to move in with any of her children for fear she might become a burden. Instead she elected to live alone in Logan in the home her second husband had left her.

Even though I had a sister in Logan, I felt both a desire and a need to help with Mom's care. I made my wishes known to the Placement Council of the Church Education System and waited for their decision. My wife and I fasted and prayed often, asking the Lord to assist us in achieving this righteous objective. But when assignments were announced for the next year, we were not asked to move. I was disappointed, but when I asked for an explanation, I was told that no move would be possible for me that year.

That summer, during meetings at BYU, I encountered the principal of the Logan Seminary, a dear friend with whom I had discussed my desire. "Ted," he asked, "why did you decide not to come to Logan?"

"I didn't decide," I told him. "The department did. I thought it was because you didn't have any openings."

"Of course we did!" he announced. "We put three brand new teachers in the Logan Seminary this year. They could have gone anywhere."

I came as close in that moment as I have ever come to shaking my fist at heaven. *I knew what was best for my mother. Didn't I?* Why hadn't the Lord given me the thing I so much desired?

A few months later, my lovely mother surrendered her independence. She moved to Orem to the home of my sister, who lived just down the street from me, less than half a mile away. Wouldn't I have had a wonderful time in Logan?

The following summer, my sister's husband accepted an assignment to serve as a mission president for three years. Ten minutes were sufficient to move Mom to her new home with us. How thankful I have been that the Lord gave me what I needed rather than what I wanted!

"It Mattereth Not Unto Me"

On a few occasions, the Lord has indicated that he does not intend to give direction in every possible circumstance. When the elders who had journeyed to Missouri by divine appointment were preparing to return to the Kirtland area, the Lord told them

I will speak unto you concerning your journey unto the land from whence you came. Let there be a craft made, or bought, as seemeth you good, *it mattereth not unto me*, and take your journey speedily for the place which is called St. Louis (D&C 60:5, 22, emphasis added).

When the prophet and his companions met a group of Elders journeying to Zion, the Lord gave them a revelation which said in part:

And now continue your journey. Assemble yourselves upon the land of Zion; and hold a meeting and rejoice together, and offer a sacrament unto the Most High. And then you may return to bear record, yea, even altogether, or two by two, as seemeth you good, *it mattereth not unto me*; only be faithful, and declare glad tidings unto the inhabitants of the earth, or among the congregations of the wicked (D&C 62:4-5, emphasis added.)

In a revelation calling Stephen Burnett on a mission in 1832, the Lord instructed

...go ye and preach my gospel, whether to the north or to the south, to the east or to the west, *it mattereth not*, for ye cannot go amiss (D&C 80:3, emphasis added).

The privilege of receiving revelation is so precious, and the promises so powerful, that we may agonize over what appears to be divine indifference or silence when we seek direction. When the answers do not come as we have hoped, we would do well to review our own worthiness. If we are prepared to receive an answer, then we ought to remember the counsel of the Lord from D&C section 58:

> For behold, it is not meet that I should command in all things; for he that is compelled in all things, the same is a slothful and not a wise servant; wherefore he receiveth no reward.
>
> Verily I say, men should be anxiously engaged in a good cause, and do many things of their own free will, and bring to pass much righteousness;
>
> For the power is in them, wherein they are agents unto themselves. And inasmuch as men do good they shall in nowise lose their reward.
>
> But he that doeth not anything until he is commanded, and receiveth a commandment with doubtful heart, and keepeth it with slothfulness, the same is damned (D&C 58:26-29).

Brigham Young gave superb counsel about the proper course of action when we are unable to determine the will of God.

If I do not know the will of my Father, and what He requires of me in a certain transaction, if I ask Him to give me wisdom concerning any requirement in life, or in regard to my own course, or that of my friends, my family, my children, or those that I preside over, and get no answer from Him, and then do the very best that my judgment will teach me, He is bound to own and honor that transaction, and He will do so to all intents and purposes (Brigham Young, *Journal of Discourses*, vol. 3, p.205).

Trusting in the Love of God

In every case we must, as we approach the Throne of Grace with our requests and our gratitude, remember the love of God for his children. Consider Job. He had ten children, and "was the greatest of all the men of the east" (Job 1:3). Four messengers came to him one day. Each arrived while the preceding one was still speaking. Their message? All Job had—his sheep, his camels, his oxen, and his asses–was gone and his children were dead. (See Job 1:13-19.) Perhaps real empathy is impossible for us in the face of such tragedies.

Even though Job was consumed by grief (Job 1:20), he said,

> Naked came I out of my mother's womb, and naked shall I return thither: the Lord gave, and the Lord hath taken away; blessed be the name of the Lord (Job 1:21).

Then the disease came. Job was so disfigured that his friends did not recognize him (Job 19:13-15). Pustulating sores in which worms or maggots bred covered his body (Job 7:5). His breath was so foul, and his body emitted such an odor, that his friends abhorred him (Job 10:17). He was covered with boils and lived with the outcasts beyond the city limits. They mocked him (Job 30:1, 5, 8-13). Pain was his constant companion (Job 30:17, 30). Things became so bad that his wife cried, "Dost thou still retain thine integrity? curse God, and die" (Job 2:9).

In one of the great statements of the Old Testament, Job responded, "What? Shall we receive good at the hand of God, and shall we not receive evil?" (Job 2:10).

If we believe that God is wise enough to know when to say "Yes" to us, then we must believe that he is wise enough to know when to say "No." We must trust him, no matter how he deals with us. Job told his friends, "Though he slay me, yet will I trust in him" (Job 13:15). Or, in other words, "If God has not given me what I want, then what he has given me is better."

A simple testimony from Nephi offers comfort when God seems to be far away, his purposes seem hard to discern, and all his answers seem to be negatives. Nephi said, "I know [God] loveth his children; nevertheless, I do not know the meaning of all things" (1 Nephi 11:17). We may not always understand what God is doing, or why, but we can always trust him. He is love (1 John 4:8).

A small blind girl demonstrated this kind of trust when she accompanied her father to visit his friend. As they were talking, the friend placed the small girl on his lap and held her. A moment later, the father realized that she might be nervous in the arms of a stranger. "Sweetheart," he said, "do you know who is holding you?"

"No," she replied, "but you do."

In a time of trial some day, someone may say to us, "Do you know why this is happening to you?" And we should respond, "No. But my Heavenly Father does."

Our responsibility is to learn to hear the answers God gives to us, and then to submit, knowing we are safe in the everlasting arms of his love.

Getting What We Pray For

Under the right circumstances, we can receive everything we pray for. There are two preliminary requirements. First, what we ask for must be right. Second, we must be right.

Consider these two conditions:

1. *WHAT WE ASK FOR MUST BE RIGHT*

A. "And whatsoever ye shall ask the Father in my name, *which is right...*" (3 Nephi 18:20, emphasis added).

B. "And now, if God...doth grant unto you whatsoever ye ask *that is right...*" (Mosiah 4:21, emphasis added).

C. "My God will give me, *if I ask not amiss...*" (2 Nephi 4:35, emphasis added).

D. "Whatsoever ye ask the Father in my name it shall be given you, *that is expedient for you*" (D&C 88:64, emphasis added).

If we come before the Father in prayer but we are not certain that the thing we request is right, then we must follow the Savior's example in Luke 22:42: "...Nevertheless not my will, but thine, be done."

So very much of pure prayer seems to be the process of discovering, rather than requesting, the will of our Father in heaven and then aligning ourselves therewith (Elder Neal A. Maxwell, *All These Things Shall Give Thee Experience*, p.93).

The Bible Dictionary of the Church's edition of the King James Version tells us that

> Prayer is the act by which the will of the Father and the will of the child are brought into correspondence with each other. The object of prayer is not to change the will of God, but to secure for ourselves and for others blessings that God is already willing to grant, but that are made conditional on our asking for them (*Bible Dictionary*, pp.752-753).

On occasion, the Lord has granted requests for things that were, perhaps, better left ungranted, in order to teach a lesson and in order to satisfy the demands of a servant who will not accept 'No' for an answer. Martin Harris, Joseph Smith, and the one hundred and sixteen pages of the Book of Mormon manuscript offer a striking illustration. (See D&C, headings for sections 3 and 10.) Martin had rendered such valuable aid to Joseph, and was under such pressure from his family, that Joseph could not bear to turn down his request to take the translated pages home in order to prove the inspiration of the work.

It was only after "much solicitation" and having "wearied the Lord in asking" that permission was finally given for the pages to be entrusted to Martin, who covenanted to show them only to a small group of relatives. Martin Harris did not keep his covenant, and the manuscript pages were lost. (See *Documentary History of the Church*, Vol. 1, pp.20-21.) Joseph shared the responsibility for the loss because he had not been willing to accept the Lord's refusal when first he sought consent. The Lord chastened Joseph for his part in the affair: "For, behold, you should not have feared man more than God" (D&C 3:7). The Lord also said, "Because you delivered up those writings...into the hands of a wicked man, you have lost them. And you have also lost your gift [to translate]" (D&C 10:1-2).

No matter how desirable a blessing seems to us, and no matter how marvelous (in our perspective), the benefits might be, we must submit to the Lord's will and the Lord's answers, lest we find ourselves, as Joseph did, in great difficulty.

Boyd K. Packer explained:

On several occasions when a member has insisted that something be done his way, I have remembered that great lesson from Church history. I have said to myself in my mind:

All right, Joseph, give the manuscript to Martin Harris. Do it your own way, and see where you get. Then when you're confounded and confused, come back and we'll get you set on the course that you might have taken earlier if you had been submissive and responsive. Someone wrote:

> *With thoughtless and impatient hands*
> *We tangle up the plans*
> *The Lord hath wrought.*
> *And when we cry in pain He saith,*
> *'Be quiet, man, while I untie the knot.'*

(Anonymous)

(*Ensign*, November 1979, p.21)

2. WE MUST BE RIGHT

A. "For the Lord hath heard thy prayers and hath *judged of thy righteousness*" (Mosiah 3:4, emphasis added).

B. "And now, if God...doth grant unto you whatso-ever ye ask that is right, *in faith, believing that ye shall receive...*" (Mosiah 4:21, emphasis added).

C. "Ask *with a sincere heart, with real intent, having faith...*" (Moroni 10:4, emphasis added).

D. "All things shall be done unto thee according to thy word, for *thou shalt not ask that which is contrary to my will*" (Helaman 10:5, emphasis added).

E. "But let him *ask in faith, nothing wavering...*"
(James 1:6, emphasis added).

Remember that the Lord may say, in answering our requests, "No" or "Not yet." If we get either of these answers, there are two possible reasons. First, what we have asked for may not be right, and a "Yes" answer might impede the plans of God for the welfare of his children. Second, we might not be right, and a "Yes" answer would do us more harm than good by teaching us incorrect principles, or reinforcing our unworthiness. It is imperative that we never lose sight of the reality that we are being proved in this mortal environment (Abraham 3:25). We should not expect God to remove all of our problems because we pray. Sometimes we must endure in faith while we pray, waiting on the will of God and knowing that whatever he is doing to us will be good for us if we are willing.

We tend to think only in terms of our endurance, but it is God's patient long-suffering which provides us with our chances to improve, affording us urgently needed developmental space or time. (See Alma 42:4-5.)

Paul observed, "Now no chastening for the present seemeth to be joyous, but grievous: nevertheless afterward it yieldeth the peaceable fruit of righteousness" (Hebrews 12:11). Such "peaceable fruit" comes only in the appointed season thereof, after the blossoms and the buds.

Otherwise, if certain mortal experiences were cut short, it would be like pulling up a flower to see how the roots are doing. Put another way, too many anxious openings of the oven door, and the cake falls instead of rising. Moreover, enforced change usually does not last, while productive enduring can ingrain permanent change. (See Alma 32:13-16; Elder Neal A. Maxwell, C.R., April 1990, p.42.)

The Prayers of the Imperfect

Some time after he had lost the one hundred and sixteen translated pages, Martin Harris desired to be one of the Three Witnesses to the Book of Mormon. He made it a matter of prayer.

The Lord had made clear to Joseph by revelation the nature of this man. He called Martin Harris a wicked man (D&C 10:1); he said that Martin had tried to destroy Joseph's gift (D&C 10:7); he indicated that Martin refused to humble himself (D&C 5:24); and confess his sins (D&C 5:28). Under these circumstances, the Lord's response was "No." Martin was not right, and the answer would not change until he got himself right:

And now, except he humble himself and acknowledge unto me the things that he has done which are
wrong, and covenant with me that he will keep my com-

mandments, and exercise faith in me, behold I say unto him, he shall have no such views, for I will grant unto him no views of the things of which I have spoken (D&C 5:28).

There is another great lesson in this story, one that has encouraged me for many years. Even though Martin was an unrepentant and disobedient man, "a wicked man," the Lord gave him an answer to his prayers through Joseph, telling Martin what he needed to do to get a "Yes" answer. However, in the event that Martin Harris was unwilling to comply with these requirements, then, said the Lord, "I command you, my servant Joseph, that you shall say unto him, that he shall do no more, *nor trouble me any more* concerning this matter" (D&C 5:29, emphasis added).

Martin's prayers *troubled* the Lord, but he did not simply tune them out or turn them off. He listened. And he responded.

This is not a unique event. In August of 1831 the Lord gave instructions to the Saints in Zion concerning the use of the resources of the earth. "This," he said, "is according to the law and the prophets; wherefore, *trouble me no more concerning this matter*" (D&C 59:22, emphasis added).

In March of 1833, the Lord spoke to the Saints in Zion again, about their apparent requests that Joseph come to live in Zion. He said, "I have called [Joseph] to preside over

Zion in mine own due time. Therefore, *let them cease weary-
ing me concerning this matter*" (D&C 90:32-33, emphasis
added).

Joseph recorded that on one occasion he was praying
very earnestly to know the time of the Second Coming
when he heard a voice:

> Joseph, my son, if thou livest until thou art eighty-
> five years old, thou shalt see the face of the Son of Man;
> therefore let this suffice, and trouble me no more on
> this matter (D&C 130:15, emphasis added).

I have on occasion imagined my Heavenly Father in a
great room, the walls covered with switches, and the
switches labeled with the names of his children. When we
are right, our switches are in the 'on' position, and Father
hears our prayers. But when we are wrong, when our lives
do not demonstrate our commitment to our covenants, the
Lord flips the switches to 'off.' For example, "Martin
Harris is a wicked man." *Click!* "The Saints in Zion have
troubled me too much about Joseph moving there." *Click!*
"The people of Ninevah are debased, depraved, and degen-
erate." *Click!* "Ted Gibbons is a terrible home teacher."
Click! But this is clearly not the way our prayers work.
Nahum said of Ninevah,

Woe to the bloody city! it is full of lies and robbery; the prey departeth not; The noise of a whip, and the noise of the rattling of the wheels, and of the prancing horses, and of the jumping chariots. The horseman lifteth up both the bright sword and the glittering spear: and there is a multitude of slain, and a great number of carcasses; and there is none end of their corpses; they stumble upon their corpses: Because of the multitude of the whoredoms of the wellfavoured harlot, the mistress of witchcraft, that selleth nations through her whoredoms, and families through her witchcrafts (Nahum 3:1-4).

The armies of Assyria, of which Ninevah was capital, were renowned for cold-blooded cruelty and sadistic terror.

The prophet Jonah was called to preach destruction to Ninevah (Jonah 3:4), but he refused and fled in the opposite direction with what seems to be good reason.

The Lord was able with the help of a big fish to persuade Jonah to go to Ninevah and preach. His message was not a recitation of the love of the Lord and a gentle invitation to repent. Rather, he announced to the people that they would be overthrown in forty days. Then, to Jonah's chagrin and amazement, these dreadful people repented, giving themselves to fasting and mighty prayer (Jonah 3:7-8). And God listened. We must not miss the meaning of this. Here was a city of one hundred and twenty thousand or more that was so wholly given to wickedness that God's messenger did not preach repentance, but destruction. But when they prayed, God listened!

Is that not comforting? Lucifer would love to convince us that our wickedness prevents the Father from hearing our prayers. Nothing could be less true! We must remember that when we pray, regardless of our attitude or worthiness or effort, our Heavenly Father is listening. Our switches are always in the 'on' position.

> I want you to know that whenever one of Heavenly Father's children kneels and talks to him, he listens. I know this as well as I know anything in this world— that Heavenly Father listens to every prayer from his children. I know our prayers ascend to heaven. No matter what we may have done wrong, he listens to us (Bishop H. Burke Peterson, *Ensign* , June 1981, p.73).

The Sensitivity of the Spirit

In the process of living in the world, all of us are subject to sin. In fact, "If we say we have no sin, we deceive ourselves..." (1 John 1:8). Thus, we may never be wholly right when we bend our knees and appeal for God's help.

Sometimes, it is in the process of prayer that we get ourselves right.

The sensitivity of the Spirit is so great that even a small, unresolved matter with a brother or a family member might prevent us from receiving answers. This is in part the meaning behind the following verses from the Sermon on the Mount:

> Therefore if thou bring thy gift to the altar, and there rememberest that thy brother hath ought against thee;
>
> Leave there thy gift before the altar, and go thy way; first be reconciled to thy brother, and then come and offer thy gift (Matthew 5:23-24).

My brother, while he was in a stake presidency, had a disagreement with a high councilor over a sister in one of the wards. Both leaders felt that she should be called to positions they were trying to fill. My brother felt certain that he had received a spiritual confirmation of his decision to call her. But when he presented the matter to the President, the high councilor admitted that he had already interviewed her and called her into the organization for which he had responsibility.

The matter was resolved, and the positions were both filled, but there remained some negative feelings.

Many months passed. The Stake President asked my brother to travel to one of the branches in the stake for the purpose of releasing the branch president and calling a new one. The above-mentioned high councilor was to go as his companion. They arrived early and began interviewing, with the intention of making the leadership change in sacrament meeting. There were several logical choices, but they could not get a confirmation. They changed the order of the meetings to give themselves more time, but the day came to an end with no new President selected. They had to return the next week.

The interviewing commenced once again and continued without progress of any kind. During a momentary break, my brother, feeling frustrated over their inability to conclude the matter, looked at his companion, remembered the conflict over the call of a sister so many months ago, and realized that he still had feelings of resentment.

With that realization, he understood the problem. He turned to the high councilor and said something like this: "You know, I never really apologized for that disagreement we had. Maybe that's why we're not getting help. I want to ask you to forgive me."

The companion expressed the same sincere feelings of apology and they returned to the process of finding the new branch president. My friend concluded, "We both had one of the richest outpourings of our experience a few moments later when we prayed about a man. The choice was clearly confirmed."

"I Did Pour Out My Whole Soul"

When we are not right, the probability of God answering our prayers in the way we desire is diminished. In fact, this is the only reasonable explanation when we pray for things which are right, yet the prayers continue for hours or days or years before an answer comes. Such prayers are not an attempt to change God but to change ourselves. Our Father is not waiting until he is inclined to answer but until the answer will be a blessing in our lives.

When Enos got himself right, answers came in finished sentences, and with promises that even now affect the descendants of Lehi (Enos 1:13).

Twelve times in the Book of Mormon a phrase appears which illuminates one means by which we make ourselves right when we pray. The phrase first occurs in Enos 1:9, where Enos says, "I did *pour out my whole soul unto God*" (emphasis added). This matter of pouring out the soul in prayer is also mentioned in Mosiah 14:12, Mosiah 24:12, Mosiah 24:21, Mosiah 26:14, Alma 19:14, Alma 34:26, Alma 46:17, Alma 58:10, Helaman 7:11, Helaman 7:14, and Mormon 3:12.

Most of our lives contain hidden chambers. We try to present to those around us, and to our Father, the appearance of near-perfect obedience, but sometimes there are areas of our lives, as there might be bottom drawers and upper shelves in a home, that need to be cleaned. Likewise, we sometimes keep back parts of our soul for our own purposes rather than surrendering them for the glory of God and the building up of Zion. It is because of this tendency that the scriptures so often repeat the injunction "Thou shalt love the Lord thy God with *all* thy heart" (Deut. 6:5). Likewise we are enjoined to have "an eye *single* to the glory of God" (D&C 4:5).

Mosiah 15:7 describes the relationship between the Father and the Son in these words: "The will of the Son being swallowed up in the will of the Father." What an honor it would be if a similar thing could be said about us. "Her will is swallowed up in the will of the Savior. Nothing leaks out. Nothing spills over the edges."

When we pour out our whole soul unto God, we pour ourselves "into the cups of our words" (Truman Madsen, *The Improvement Era*, February 1966, p.158). We continue pouring until we have poured all of ourselves out, until we have emptied the hidden chambers, until we have mastered our will and made ourselves submissive to the will of the Father and the Son; until we are purified. Then the answers come. D&C 50:29 says, "And if ye are purified and cleansed from all sin, ye shall ask whatsoever you will in the name of Jesus and it shall be done."

The promise of this verse is sobering, for it teaches that it is possible to get everything we ask for. You will probably remember the promise made to Nephi, the son of Helaman, that "all things shall be done unto thee according to thy word," which promise was made because the will of Nephi was swallowed up in the will of the Father and the Son. The Lord explained, "For thou shalt not ask that which is contrary to my will" (Helaman 10:5).

In simplest terms, all that is necessary for us to get everything we pray for is for us to accomplish the following:

1. We must be right. We must submit ourselves to the will of the Father and purify ourselves.

2. We must ask for those things that are right, and we can know, in advance, which things are right, if we are inspired by the Holy Spirit in our requests:

A. He that asketh in the Spirit asketh according to the will of God; wherefore it is done even as he asks (D&C 46:30).

B. And if ye are purified and cleansed from all sin, ye shall ask whatsoever you will in the name of Jesus and it shall be done. But know this, it shall be given you [you shall be inspired in] what you shall ask (D&C 50:29-30).

C. ...and they did not multiply many words, for it was given them what they should pray, and they were filled with desire (3 Nephi 19:24).

This does not mean that prayers are answered only for the perfect. The closer we come to perfection the less probable it is that what we ask for will be withheld. Perfection is not a requirement. What is required is that we be prepared in such a way that an affirmative answer will not damage our spirituality or our concept of the nature of God and his expectations of his children. We must also be patient as we wait on the will of the Lord.

Help from the Lord generally comes in increments. He can immediately cure serious illnesses or disabilities or even allow the dead to be raised. But the general pattern is that improvement comes in sequential steps. That plan gives us an opportunity to discover what the Lord expects us to learn. It requires our patience to recognize His timetable. It provides growth from our efforts and trust in Him and the opportunity to express gratitude for the help given (Richard G. Scott, "Obtaining Help from the Lord," *Ensign*, Nov. 1991, p.85).

⧉⧉

"And Yet Thou Art There"

Chapter 11

When I was little, I wanted to be Aladdin. I dreamed of magic lamps and genies and three wishes. Those days are past, but I have not been disappointed. I have a Father and God who framed the universe and filled it with worlds without number (Moses 1:33); who set the stars in the heavens (Job 38:31-33); and gave them light (D&C 88:9); a being of immeasurable ability and limitless love who listens to me and answers me. And as I make my will conform to his and seek his help, he opens to me the storehouses of his wisdom and power and goodness. And his bounty does not end after three gifts.

I pray that all of you...will remember that you can get just as close to your Heavenly Father as you can to your earthly father, if you will undertake to live righteously, to talk to him regularly, and to keep his commandments (Hugh B. Brown, *The Improvement Era*, June 1967, p.96).

He Is Kind, Forever

It is a boundless blessing to be able to talk at any time with an omnipotent and omniscient being who loves us, who blesses us, who weeps over us, and who will converse with us.

Enoch described the greatness of God in these words:

And were it possible that man could number the particles of the earth, yea, millions of earths like this, it would not be a beginning to the number of thy creations.... (Moses 7:30).

Yet in the midst of this magnificence and creative splendor, the honest seeker can always find God, the Father:

...and yet thou art there, and thy bosom is there; and also thou art just; thou art merciful and kind forever (Moses 7:30, emphasis added).

I have learned that he is there. In the midst of an incomprehensible number of creations, I have always been able to find him. And I have learned that Enoch was correct. He is just and merciful and kind—so very kind—forever.

෯ ෯

About the Author

Ted Gibbons was born and raised in Logan, Utah. After serving a mission to Brazil, he attended Utah State University on a theater arts scholarship. He graduated with a degree in both speech and education. In 1968 he married the former Lydia Kimball, then was inducted into military service. He was the Distinguished Military Graduate of his class, and after two years he reached the rank of captain.

Ted returned from the service to enter BYU to begin a Masters program, and after one term was hired by the Church Educational System to teach seminary in Phoenix. During three years at Arizona State University, he completed his Masters in audio visual education and was transferred to Snowflake, Arizona where he served as seminary principal for four years. In 1980, after returning from the Church Educational System's tour of Israel, Ted moved his family to Orem, Utah, where he began work on a Doctoral degree in Instructional Science at BYU. After two years in Orem on sabbatical and teaching at BYU, he was assigned to teach seminary at Pleasant Grove High School. He became principal there and later at MountainView

Seminary in Orem. He is presently teaching at the Orem Institute of Religion.

In addition to his church assignments, he has participated for many years in the *Know Your Religion* program. He has presented hundreds of times over the past several years his one-man stage presentation of *Sealing the Testimony: Willard Richards' Eyewitness Account of the Martyrdom*. He is a published author of numerous books and articles, and was the co-lyricist of *Rabboni* an Easter cantata performed by the Tabernacle Choir.

Ted and his wife, Lydia, are the parents of twelve children.